*T*raveling
with
Hermes

Traveling with Hermes

HERMENEUTICS and RHETORIC

Bruce Krajewski

The University of Massachusetts Press / Amherst

Copyright © 1992 by
The University of Massachusetts Press
All rights reserved
Printed in the United States of America
LC 92-5080
ISBN 0-87023-815-9
Designed by Jack Harrison
Set in Adobe Garamond by Keystone Typesetting, Inc.
Printed and bound by Thomson-Shore, Inc.

Library of Congress Cataloging-in-Publication Data
Krajewski, Bruce, 1959–
     Traveling with Hermes : hermeneutics and rhetoric / Bruce Krajewski.
        p.   cm.
     Includes bibliographical references and index.
     ISBN 0-87023-815-9 (alk. paper)
     1. Criticism. 2. Rhetoric. 3. Hermeneutics. I. Title.
PN81.K69   1992
801'.95—dc20   92-5080
                                                        CIP

British Library Cataloguing in Publication data are available.

Frontispiece: Jan Steen, *Rhetoricians at a Window.*
The John G. Johnson Collection, Philadelphia Museum of Art.

for
Mark Hochstrasser
kalos

Voices. Voices. Listen, my heart, as only
saints have listened: until the gigantic call lifted them
off the ground; yet they kept on, impossibly,
kneeling and didn't notice at all:
so complete was their listening. Not that you could endure
God's voice—far from it. But listen to the voice of the wind
and the ceaseless message that forms itself out of silence.

—Rainer Maria Rilke, *Duino Elegies*

Contents

Acknowledgments

An earlier version of "Postmodernism, Allegory, and Hermeneutics in *Brazil*," appeared in "Modernism and Postmodernism," *Annals of Scholarship* 6, nos. 2–3 (1989). My thanks to Ruth Graham for her patience and for her permission.

I would like to thank the University of Iowa for its support. The University of Chicago provided me with a postdoctoral fellowship, which gave me time to revise and to send the manuscript off. The staff at Regenstein Library were especially helpful. Although I have been at Laurentian University but a short time, everyone here has been generous and supportive.

Writing and language are not one's own. Among other things, one hears voices, influences. Gerald Bruns initiated me into hermeneutics, transformed me from a Neo-Kantian into what might be called a Gadamerian. Knowing him has changed my life. Don Marshall has stuck by me from the beginning, even when my stupidity must have been exasperating. Don is a model scholar and an august man. Katherine Hayles has been a splendid reader, and rightly chided me for rash judgments about Derrida and about science. David Klemm, Dudley Andrew, and Huston Diehl offered friendly criticisms. Geoff Waite took my work seriously before its time.

Of course, many friends contributed to this project, which means they have contributed to my life as well. Dan Rockwell, Caryl Flinn, Jane Jeffrey, Brian Shaffer, Shannon Hengen, Virginia Dummitt, Hilary Siebert, Linda Berberoglu, Annie Wilcox, Bill Freeman, Bob Grunst, Paul Van Dyke, Scot Wilcox, Sarah Witte, Sherry Ceniza, Bernadette Korndorf, Robin Hochstrasser. I trust that all of these people will realize that this brief acknowledgment is not meant to account for the years of friendship they have given me.

Bob Wallace and David Adams, who also helped with the book, are relatively new friends, and I hope we will become old ones.

Clark Dougan amazed me from the first moment with his care and encouragement. I could not have hoped for a better editor. My thanks also to Carol Schoen at the Press for her help.

Mark Hochstrasser inspired this work, and he continues to bring the world to life. He is a gift from the gods, and a friend in the way Emerson describes: "a musical & permeable angel."

$\mathcal{T}$raveling
with
Hermes

*R*hetoricians at a Window

Recently, it seems, some of my colleagues have been trying to "save my soul" from such dishonest things as rhetoric! They think that hermeneutics is no noble pursuit and that we must be suspicious of rhetoric. I had to reply that rhetoric has been the basis of our social life since Plato rejected and contradicted the flattering abuse of rhetoric by the Sophists. He introduced dialectically founded rhetoric as in the *Phaedrus,* and rhetoric remained a noble art throughout antiquity. Yet one wonders why today everybody is not aware of it.—Hans-Georg Gadamer[1]

In the midst of this disintegrating world appear the rhétoriqueurs, each in his own way tormented by a conscious inability to know the world or express it in suitable terms.—Paul Zumthor[2]

It is certain that quacks habitually collaborated with Rederijkers.
—Albert Heppner[3]

If you want a frame for this work, you might look at the frontispiece, Jan Steen's painting *Rhetoricians at a Window,* where the rhetoricians are not in a hothouse, nor in an enclosed environment, but out in the open.[4] The viewer is at street level, and the rhetoricians are leaning out toward the viewer. Completed sometime during the 1660s, Steen's work is but one of many he did on the *rederijkers,* the rhetoricians who played a large part in popular entertainment in the Netherlands. As Heppner explains, "The *Rederijkers* were organised throughout the Netherlands in 'kamers' or chambers, which were in touch with one another and gave joint performances, such as dramatic competitions" (PTR, 22). By nature, and perhaps by occupation in this case, rhetoricians are social

3

creatures. Steen apparently was a friend to a group of *rederijkers,* inasmuch as painters often helped with the scenery for the *rederijkers'* dramatic performances (PTR, 23).

Six figures are near the window. Among them are a robust man closely attending to a text, as if he needed light to make out the dark characters; some people in a darkened background, perhaps representative of the sinister side of rhetoric; and someone with a gesture of delight, or perhaps of insight, who is smiling. Some of these figures converge at a liminal point—the window, a place that opens out on to something larger. Think of the open window in connection with the talk of the open hand of rhetoric as opposed to the closed fist of logic. If nothing else, Steen's painting could be said to exhibit the social nature of rhetoric, for it is not a rhetorician at a window, but rhetoricians; a solitary rhetorician would be an oddity. In the many paintings of rhetoricians that Steen produced, all involve groups, and several times he depicts them at a window. Furthermore, the blazon hanging from the window displays an emblem of a particular *rederijker* group. The emblem consists of crossed pipes and a wineglass, which are underneath an inscription that reads, "the green laurel shoot." The emblem tells us that the *rederijkers* were "as much social as literary" (BP, 26).

The vine around the window "probably alludes to the *rederijkers'* love of the grape" (BP, 26). In other words, the rhetoricians are not overly concerned with self-possession, and perhaps would be more likely to appreciate Alcibiades than Socrates. This connection reminds us of a basic distinction between philosophy and rhetoric—or if you prefer, between philosophy and poetry—that philosophers since Socrates have wanted to draw: poets are possessed, while philosophers are self-possessed. The classic example here is Ion, who, while not possessed by drink, claims to be possessed by the Muses as he recites poetry—which means that he cannot account for how he knows what he knows. During the questioning, Ion comes out looking silly, as if those who cannot account for knowing how they know do not count. Similarly, to *know* that you do not know—Socratic wisdom—does not come off much better. I suppose this is why many become angry at the Socrates of the *Apology,* who rigorously insists on his knowledge of not knowing, and who refuses to play a tragic role at his trial. Instead, he makes jokes and wisecracks, he mocks the jurors, and one can almost imagine him winking to his friends.

It is silly to say the comic lacks seriousness, but that is just the case. Silliness needs rethinking, if only to consider why it is etymologically related to the holy. Bruns comments that "the task of comedy, after all, is to elude greatness and to accept the ordinary. . . ."[5] The history of rhetoricians does not result in a list of great names that everyone would recognize, which is in striking contrast to what the history of philosophers gives you. Rhetoricians dirty their hands in the familiar—in law courts, in political battles, in popular entertainment—so that it seems to me off the mark that people like Brian Vickers, in his *In Defence of Rhetoric*,[6] want to elevate rhetoric out of the mud, to look at rhetoricians not near street level as Steen shows the *rederijkers,* but to look *up* to them. The rest of this text is about Hans-Georg Gadamer's efforts to move us to look rhetoric in the eye, and risk sullying our purity in relation to the grave. One begins to understand rhetoric when one begins to appreciate that the *rederijkers* habitually associated with quacks.

Some of my colleagues cannot bother themselves with hermeneutics and rhetoric, because they are busy moving "beyond" hermeneutics, putting as much distance as possible between themselves and the unsavory and questionable practices of rhetoricians. Some who do bother themselves make sure they point out that the activities of understanding (hermeneutics) and persuasion (rhetoric) smack of imperialism, given that the activities seek to make what is alien familiar. One response I give is to point to the work of Emmanuel Levinas, who frequently addresses one's relationship with the Other. It seems to me that Levinas does not speak of dominating or subjugating the Other. In fact, the encounter with the Other leads to a reversal of what imperialism watchers expect; that is, that the meeting with the Other puts you in question, makes you realize that you are a "hostage." Levinas says, "The greatest intimacy of me to myself consists in being at every moment responsible for the others, the hostage of others."

This project began out of wonderment about the intertwined relationship of hermeneutics and rhetoric, which Gadamer mentions briefly in "On the Scope and Function of Hermeneutical Reflection."[7] Later, I was introduced to other pieces in which Gadamer speaks of hermeneutics and rhetoric together, such as "*Die Ausdruckskraft der Sprache*" and *Rhetorik und Hermeneutik*.[8] Much remains to be done, if only to persuade others that such a relationship exists.

CHAPTER ONE

Simple Hermeneutics of "The Purloined Letter"

People travel a long distance to be able to say:
This reminds me of some other place.
—Yehuda Amichai

All propaganda or popularization involves a putting of the complex into the simple, but such a move is instantly destructive, for if the complex *can* be put into the simple then it is not as complex as it seemed in the first place; and if the simple can be an adequate medium of such complexity, then it cannot, after all, be as simple as all that. A mutual transference of qualities between simple and complex takes place, forcing us to revise our initial estimate of both terms and to ponder the possibility that a translation of the one into the other was made possible only by virtue of a secret complicity between them.—Terry Eagleton[1]

I

Hermeneutics is a very old practice. The word "hermeneutics" derives from the Greek verb *hermeneuein*. As Heidegger explains, the verb is related to the noun *hermeneus*, which is referable to the god Hermes, the divine messenger. Since Hermes communicates with the gods, he brings the message of destiny; *hermeneuein* is that exposition which brings tidings because it can listen to a message. *Hermeneuein* means to bring what is hidden out into the open; it means to interpret.

Given that Hermes carried words from the gods, his messages were often oracular, ambiguous, strange, and his appearance was not always welcome—he was said to lead the souls into the underworld at death.[2] Hermes invented language and speech. In the

Cratylus, Socrates points out that Hermes could be called interpreter or messenger, but also thief, liar, or contriver. Socrates says that words—Hermes' invention—have the power to reveal, but also to conceal and to withhold. Speech can signify almost anything and turn things this way and that. Indeed, we can never get a grasp on words, hold them still, fix them (as if there were something wrong with them). Words' meanings always change, because contexts are always changing. It is in the *Cratylus* that Hermes begins to receive a tainted reputation.

It is appropriate that Hermes is associated with hermeneutics, because he is a messenger, someone whose existence and purpose depend on dialogue. He takes messages from goddess to god, or from the goddesses and gods to mortals; he is the embodiment and movement of discourse. "From the side of hermeneutics, we can say that to understand anything means to enter into a dialogue with it."[3] Dialogue is the give and take between two, the question and the response, the circular movement. That dialogue is primary to understanding shows that understanding is a social, not a private, act, nor a mental operation. Thus Wittgenstein's statement that there is no such thing as a private language. (Wittgenstein also notes the importance—for understanding—of what is not plain, not quotidian: "How does one know straight off that it makes sense to say 'Perhaps everything strikes this person as unreal [*unwirklich*], although he never speaks of it'? Of course I have here purposely chosen a very rare experience. For because it is not one of the everyday experiences, one looks more sharply at the use of words.")[4]

Dialogue as a way to achieve understanding between people can be reasonably accepted, but we want to ask the question, How do you enter into a dialogue with a text? Let me offer some words from the Russian critic V. N. Volosinov, who says that dialogue is not only "direct face-to-face vocalized verbal communication between persons, but also verbal communication of any type whatever. A book, that is, a verbal performance in print, is also an element of verbal communication."[5]

This part about books as an element of a dialogue is strange (a clue to its importance). What do you say to a book? Well, you always have questions about a text: What does it mean? Who is its author? Why was it written? Who put it in the marketplace? What question does this text answer? Why is the text constructed in this manner? As in the Platonic dialogues, the dialogue with a text begins with questioning, and the text can answer some of those questions; it can speak to you, and thus be a partner in the dialogue. Furthermore, Gadamer says that there is the question the text puts to us (we are called into question), a point that often gets overlooked when critics seek to demonstrate their superiority to the text.

Perhaps this concept of reader and text as partners in dialogue can be better understood through the insights of Paul Ricoeur. He says, "What must be interpreted in a text is a proposed world which I could inhabit and wherein I could project one of my own most possibilities. This is what I call the world of the text, the world proper to this unique text."[6] The text proposes a way of being in the world. (Might a variation of Wittgenstein be appropriate here? A text's meaning depends on its usage?) Ricoeur emphasizes that appropriation, which I will address in a moment, is a key part of hermeneutics, and that ultimately, what you appropriate is that proposed world of the text. "That world is *not behind* the text, as a hidden intention would be, but *in front of* it, as that which the work unfolds, discovers, reveals."[7] This shows the difference between hermeneutics and the hermeneutics of suspicion.

A good example of this sort of appropriation is film. To carry through with Ricoeur's image, we could imagine ourselves standing in the light from a projector (one must activate the projector oneself) that is showing some film, say *The Maltese Falcon.* We would not be a shadow in that world, but a participant, perhaps Sam Spade's friend. This conflicts with the idea of a "close reading," because to be close to the beam is still to be outside of the projected world. You must enter the world. To understand is to be let *in* on something, so you let yourself go in to the projected world, something like Alice stepping through the Looking Glass. Even if you are close, you are still an outsider, on your side of the looking glass, and the text remains an object, for there remains a distance between you and the text. (Remember what happens in Buster Keaton's *Sherlock,*

Jr., and in Woody Allen's *The Purple Rose of Cairo,* a mingling of worlds.) The idea of the dialogue also suggests something other than a critical reading, for a critical reading removes the possibility of dialogue. Can you enter into an equal dialogue with someone or something that has got you under analysis?[8]

What you do when you allow the text to speak to you is to make its meaning real for you, to appropriate the text, to make it your own. When you make a text your own, you are able to tell someone else what the text has to say, and it might have to say more than you can say. You can account for it, in part. You make your own what was initially alien. The aim of all hermeneutics is to struggle against cultural distance and historical alienation, with the emphasis on struggle, for hermeneutical experience tends not toward comfort but toward the tragic. Interpretation renders experience contemporary and similar, or in Wittgenstein's words, it helps things "hang together." In effect, the past appears through a text (though the past appears in other ways) and has something to say to you as reader, and you listen, take in what it says, and respond.[9]

Here again we see the give and take, the speaking and the listening, the to-and-fro movement of appropriation. As Gadamer says, this to-and-fro movement is like play.[10] Think of play as a way to appropriation, for play is the performance of movement. When you read a text, you are receiving an invitation to undergo an imaginative variation of your ego. The Looking Glass beckons Alice to move, to enter. She is not to remain outside, staring at herself in the Looking Glass. Her task is to stop seeing only herself, to lose herself by stepping through the mirror. Ricoeur says, "As reader, I find myself only by losing myself." Like Alice, after you are in the world of the text, you are no longer the same. Likewise, play is an experience which transforms those who participate in it. For instance, there is a curious lack of decisiveness in the playing consciousness, which makes it impossible to decide between belief and nonbelief. Gadamer says that "play fulfills its purpose only if the player loses himself in play."[11] Here, play is serious, and Claude Richard says, "The basis of modernity is the seriousness of playfulness."[12] Think of Wittgenstein's "language games."

What does this have to do with a work of art, a text? According to Gadamer, "The work of art has its true being in the fact that it becomes an experience that changes the person who experiences it. The 'subject' of the experience of art, that which remains and endures, is not the subjectivity of the person who experiences it but the work itself. This is the point at which the mode of being of play becomes significant. For play has its own essence, independent of the consciousness of those who play. . . . The players are not the subjects of play; instead play merely reaches presentation through the players."[13] Similarly, a text can reach presentation only through a player, a participant, a reader, one who is willing to be hermeludical.

Another part of appropriation involves what is called the hermeneutical circle, something hermeneutics appropriated from ancient rhetoric, which describes how understanding and interpretation, part and whole, are related in a circular way: in order to understand the parts, it is necessary to have some comprehension of the whole. As one might guess, some see this as a vicious circle from which one will never escape (see John D. Schaeffer's *Sensus Communis,* for example). The loop discussed here probably looks like a Möbius strip, and if one could experience the movement of the loop, it might feel like walking on the stairs of an Escher building, where going up and going down are not easily distinguishable.

Gadamer has described the hermeneutical circle as the interplay of the movement of tradition and the movement of the interpreter. Interpretation is conditioned by tradition and is necessarily rooted in a historical situation. How might we be conditioned by tradition? Our understanding is conditioned by the historical accumulation of previous interpretations, by the history of things themselves, and as Jürgen Habermas points out, by those who control the production and distribution of texts. *King Lear* offers an example of a way the accumulation of interpretations affects us. We pay attention to *King Lear* because our ancestors have told us it is a great drama. But we do not take *Lear* to be a play representing a unique form, for we know that many tragedies preceded it. To recognize tradition is to understand that we are in history, and that history, which is mediated by texts, has a claim on us. Since history is always changing, and since interpreters change over time through increased experience, we can say that we are always understanding differently, which explains why our understanding of *Lear* differs from that of a seventeenth-century interpreter. History offers precedents for new interpretations, just as laws are altered according to new circumstances. If you think of the law as a text, you see that the law is not static, but fluid, changeable, and you see that laws are applied differently in time. The issue of precedents brings up Gadamer's point that in order to understand the past, one must try to comprehend one's own presuppositions and prejudgments and realize how they mediate one's perception.

Consider Swift's "A Modest Proposal." One reader could be horrified at Swift's suggestion of infanticide and ignore the possibility of didactic irony. Another reader, familiar with the politics of Swift's time and with Swift's writings on other social issues, might have a different reaction to the text, in part because that reader could historically reconstruct the context. I am not privileging one reading over the other, but merely pointing out that both readings are possible, two different readings among others.

Are these readings valid? For that matter, what makes *this* text valid? These questions sound strange to a hermeneuticist, given that questions of validity presuppose that some methodology can be employed to obtain proof. Establishing rigorous proofs and syllogistic arguments is more like the work of the natural sciences than the human ones. Actually, Gadamer prefers not to be "scientific" at all. Instead, he brings in rhetoric, which concerns itself with the *eikos,* the probable. He says in "On the Scope and Function of Hermeneutical Reflection": "Where, indeed, but to rhetoric should the theoretical examination of interpretation turn? Rhetoric from oldest tradition has been the only advocate of a claim to truth that defends the probable, the *eikos* (*verisimile*), and that which is convincing to the ordinary reason, against the claim of science to accept as true only what can be demonstrated and tested! Convincing and persuading, without being able to prove—these are obviously as much the aim and measure of understanding and interpretation as they are the aim and measure of oration and persuasion."[14] Without adhering to notions of proof and validity, how can Gadamer posit a concept of truth? He historicizes and socializes truth in the manner of Wittgenstein, who, when talking about proofs in his *Remarks on the Foundations of Mathematics,* says: "I go through the proof and then accept its result. —I mean: this is simply what we do. This is use and custom among us, or a fact of our natural history."[15] Of course, the "we" here is problematic (what isn't?), but the main point is the connection between truth, history, and the *sensus communis.* Is it true that the truth of things lies in their history? For Gadamer, the true meaning of the text (the expanded notion of the a text is meant here, not just literary texts) is essentially relative to a changing horizon of discourse: "The true meaning of a text or a work of art is never finished; it is in fact an infinite process. Not only are fresh sources of error constantly excluded, so that all kinds of things are filtered out that obscure the true meaning; but new sources of understanding are continually emerging that reveal un-suspected elements of meaning. . . . This filtering process is not fixed, but is itself undergoing constant movement and extension."[16] If the truth of a thing lies in its history, then it would seem that only someone who views history as a totality could have the final say on what that thing truly meant—a God's-eye view. Gadamer is not out to supply a method for understanding; his project is to look and see how understanding works, not judge how it should work. However, this is not an opening for the claim that "anything goes," for Gadamer would contest any ahistorical methodologies, such as logical proofs.

Validity is not the same thing as truth or insight, for validity is a process, not an experience. Insight is something like the *Aha-Erlebnis,* the reaction of understanding, mentioned in Lacan's essay on the mirror stage.[17] Also, this understanding is social, as Gada-mer's appeal to rhetoric suggests. Gadamer would agree with Domi-nick LaCapra that "rhetoric involves a dialogical understanding of a discourse and of 'truth' itself in contrast to a monological idea of a unified authorial voice providing an ideally exhaustive and defini-tive (total) account of a fully mastered object of knowledge."[18]

While hermeneuticists attend to history, to the movement of being and time, they do not have a particular politics, as far as I can tell, nor have they aligned themselves with any particular political party, as have many non-Western Marxist critics. Rarely does Gadamer make overtly political statements, but an important exception is his essay, "Notes on Planning for the Future."[19] Part of the reason for this lack of attachment to a single political program stems from the absence of posited *telos* in hermeneutics. The hermeneutical circle, like Emerson's circles, will expand as long as history does, or perhaps as long as human history does. For Gadamer, understanding has no endpoint. Temporality produces change, which will call for understanding, though I find it troubling that hermeneuticists seldom talk about people shaping changes that might not occur otherwise in the flow of time. It is one thing to have *Verstehen* about slavery, and another to abolish it. Perhaps one is contingent on the other. But since some hermeneuticists would rather talk about theory than about theory's relation to community issues, theory sometimes loses its connection to the world, to the present.

Gadamer talks about the *theoros* in *Truth and Method*:

Theoros means someone who takes part in a delegation to a festival. Such a person has no other distinction or function than to be there. Thus the *theoros* is a spectator in the proper sense of the word, since he participates in the solemn act through his presence at it and thus sacred law accords him a distinction: for example: inviolability. . . . Being present has the character of being outside oneself. In the *Phaedrus* Plato already described the blunder of those who take the viewpoint of rational reasonableness and tend to misinterpret the ecstatic condition of being outside oneself, seeing it as a mere negation of being composed within oneself and hence as a kind of madness. In fact, being outside oneself is the positive possibility of being wholly with something else. This kind of being present is a self-forgetfulness, and to be a spectator consists in giving oneself in self-forgetfulness to what one is watching. Here self-forgetfulness is anything but a private condition, for it arises from devoting one's full attention to the matter at hand, and this is the spectator's own positive accomplishment.[20]

Someone who wanted to poke fun at this description might say that Chauncey Gardener from Jerzy Kosinski's *Being There* would make the ideal *theoros,* someone who has completely surrendered his attention to the spectacle that is television. I would agree that a critic's "being there" is not enough, for some balance between *logos* and *ergon,* word and deed, should be reached. Gadamer implicitly agrees with this elsewhere, in his essay on Plato's *Lysis.*[21]

What I am about to propose concerning *theoroi* is not meant to refute Gadamer's comments, since he is using the *theoros* as an example for his argument about participation, and on the overcoming of the subject/object dichotomy through involvement and dialectic. Instead, I want to enlarge upon what Gadamer says about the *theoros,* what it meant to be a *theoros,* in order to suggest some things about present theoretical practice.

Theoroi were not passive at the festivals, but offered sacrifices in the name of their cities. Thus, the same title was given to the envoys that a city sent to a distant shrine to offer sacrifices in its name, and to the envoys it sent to consult oracles. In addition, the *theoroi* served as announcers for forthcoming celebrations and festivals.[22] In our own time, theorists do not seem to represent any constituency, and they cannot announce, because they do not even attempt to speak the language of "ordinary" people. Geoffrey Hartman has taken up this matter in his book *Minor Prophecies,* and he notes that much current criticism "tends to see through texts rather than with them." Now, it seems, theorists do not serve an integrative role, but one of fragmentation, splitting off theory from life, from the community. A social theory of knowledge and of understanding, such as Wittgenstein's, Bakhtin's, Arendt's, or Gadamer's, offers an opportunity for theorists to participate once again, to counter fragmentation through dialogue.

To use a variation of a question Socrates often asked students of rhetoricians in Plato's dialogues: What will your theorist or your theory make of you? That is, what kind of human being will emerge from following a certain theorist, from taking up a particular theoretical position? The followers of philosophical hermeneutics, with its appeal to practical reason, dialogue, openness, and participation, will probably be quite different from those who choose to take up what Gadamer calls "the hermeneutics of suspicion."[23]

The next section will consider two such teachers of suspicion—
Jacques Lacan and Jacques Derrida.

II

Attending to Gadamer's insistence on historicizing, I want to consider matters in a chronological order, beginning with Lacan's 1956
"Seminar on 'The Purloined Letter.'" I will then address both
Jacques Derrida's response to Lacan in Derrida's "Le facteur de la
vérité" and Barbara Johnson's intervention in this debate in her
article, "The Frame of Reference: Poe, Lacan, Derrida."[24] There-
after, I will consider something in Poe's text that Lacan, Derrida,
and Johnson bypass, namely, the quotation that begins "The Purloined Letter," and then I will offer some criticisms of the debate
mentioned above. Next, I will explore how hermeneutics might
appropriate Poe's text in order to further our understanding about
what has been called Romantic hermeneutics. Finally, I will offer an
example of how "we" might appropriate Poe's text for present
political purposes.

I intend to practice hermeneutical heteroglossia, to allow many
voices to speak, especially feminist voice(s), since hermeneutics
has traditionally not been attractive to women, with such notable
exceptions as Hannah Arendt, Susan Handelman, and Georgia
Warnke. (Although Barbara Johnson presents an implicit feminist
critique of Lacan and Derrida's readings of Poe's text, I prefer, for
the moment, to simplify things, to make her argument explicit, and
to reinforce it, harmonize it, with the voice of Luce Irigaray. Since
feminists are obviously fragmented, the female voices in this text are
not meant to represent all of feminist thought.) In other words, I
want to bring new partners into this conversation about Poe's text.
Not all voices can speak at once, nor are the selected voices that are
to speak representative of all possible conversations that could take
place concerning "The Purloined Letter." Whereas I cannot account for all possible voices, or all potential counterarguments or
questions, what I can do is assay what can be said in this particular
case. What will appear is the kind of rhetorical criticism that is

hermeneutical, the kind that does not try to prove things through methodological rigor or to support every shaky assertion with a flying buttress, in the hope of building a Critical Cathedral that will stand for centuries. Rather, one speaks to the matter at hand, in the hope of saying something persuasive and substantial—perhaps even true. As Bruns notes, this is not the sort of criticism to offer to "an audience who wants its criticism in the form of methodological combat. . . . If it seems to you that there is something disreputable about such criticism as a rhetorician will practice, you are certainly right. It will appear to many that such criticism fails by desiring no results, only talk, when results are what we need, for they are the index of our proceedings and the assurance that we are getting somewhere. But the rhetorician does not desire to get anywhere: this is the primary meaning of his disregard of method."[25] To modify Bruns's statement a bit, I do want to get somewhere in this essay— traditionally, rhetoricians are nomads—but in order to travel, I cannot carry the Critical Cathedral on my back.

Before moving on, let me make clear some of my prejudices. Gadamer's position is decidedly different from Lacan and Derrida's, though Gadamer and Derrida might be considered allies at times. As this chapter proceeds, a reader is likely to come to the generalization that the text is about the debate among hermeneutics, psychoanalysis, deconstruction, and feminism more so than about Poe's story, which serves as kind of host. I agree with Geoff Waite that the question of the identity of the literary text—or, in this particular case, the identity and function of the letter in Poe's story—is, at times, irrelevant. Furthermore, to use Waite's words, "The very question of the identity of the text . . . already occludes access to what is, in the last instance, the more significant question, namely the ideological and political identifications of the question and questioner."[26] In other words, to return to Gadamer's description of the role of the ancient *theoroi,* are we *theoroi* who all converge at the same site representing others for the good of all? One could say that I am giving a frame to the presentation, which is to look at the matter in a negative, necessarily parasitical way (Can anything except God not be a parasite?), and this frame, as Barbara Johnson illustrates, will implicate me: "Just as the author of a criminal frame transfers guilt from himself [sic] to another by leaving signs which he hopes will be read as insufficiently erased traces or referents left by the other, the authors of any critique are themselves framed by their own frame of the other, no matter how guilty or innocent the other may be" (FR, 492). This is a particularly apt analogy for much critical writing at present, because all critics are guilty of not being able to represent all viewpoints of all groups. But I will not be implicated through implication, but through explication, through a folding out. To tell a story is to exercise power, and the "story" I have told and am about to tell will, I hope, give more energy (not exactly power) to hermeneutics.

Why "The Purloined Letter"? It is an appropriate text to consider here, for it is a site on which specific, historically determined political struggles have been and continue to be waged—between Lacan and Derrida, for instance. My purpose here, among others, is to test out ways—or if a reader prefers, "readings"—by which to activate Poe's text for present unifying action, which seems to be in keeping with Gadamer's notion of *applicatio*. Gadamer says, "The text, whether law or gospel, if it is to be understood properly—i.e., according to the claim it makes—must be understood at every moment, in every concrete situation, in a new and different way. Understanding here is always application."[27] Lacan and Derrida have applied the text for their own particular purposes—to demonstrate psychoanalysis and deconstruction. And now I hope to gain more understanding of "The Purloined Letter" by appropriating it to advance both philosophical hermeneutics and a particular group of people—people who, for now, I will call "simple folks."

I will not offer a complete summary of Lacan and Derrida's articles. Those looking for an "objective" summary of the debate can find it in *Modern Literary Theory*.[28] However, a few comments need to be made about these articles. In Lacan's psychoanalytic reading, the purloined letter becomes synonymous with the unconscious, a signifier of unconscious desire. Moreover, Lacan believes that there is a message, or a truth, to "The Purloined Letter": "The sender . . . receives from the receiver his own message in reverse form. . . . A letter always arrives at its destination" [SPL, 72]. Thus, Lacan fathoms the text and serves up a statement of a psychoanalytic lesson. On the other hand, Derrida plumbs Poe's text and discovers deconstruction, "the game of doubles, divisibility without end, textual references from fac-simile to fac-simile, the framing of frames, the interminable supplementarity of the quotation marks, the insertion of "The Purloined Letter" into a purloined letter . . ." [FV, 492–93]. Derrida does not serve up any truth, for Poe's text offers no truth for him, no ground on which truth can stand. Everything is in infinite regress, though Derrida does say elsewhere that he believes in truth. Yet, this is the "truth" for deconstructionists in some odd sense—that the truth is muddled, mottled, and mazelike, and will not serve as the end of interpretation. Derrida practices what Geoffrey Hartman calls a "hermeneutics of indeterminacy."[29] In the end, "The Purloined Letter" serves as a host for Lacan and Derrida to demonstrate that on one day the tale is about Lacan's methodology, and on another day, before a different audience, an example of Derrida's methodology, though I am willing to be persuaded that deconstruction can be a practice. What Lacan and Derrida do with Poe looks like hermeneutical appropriation. My objections to them lie elsewhere, both in what they present and ignore in Poe's text. It is these presences and absences to which I now turn.

Lacan's and Derrida's interpretations, at least from my perspective, are very subtle and complex, certainly opaque material for most people outside the academy, or outside the profession of psychiatry. In short, these are not readings for the masses—a point to which I will return in a moment. What puzzles me about these sophisticated readings is that despite their extremely "close reading," both have overlooked the epigraph that begins "The Purloined Letter," which reads, "*Nil sapientiae odiosius acumine nimio*" ["Nothing is more detestable to wisdom than too much subtlety"]. It seems paradoxical that the very first thing, the beginning, the "origin" of the story is overlooked, much in the manner the police overlook the purloined letter. With all their subtlety, Lacan and Derrida are blind to the obvious. On the other hand, the nature of rhetoric and hermeneutics is exoteric rather than esoteric, since persuasion and understanding seek to win over people, to create peers, rather than to divide people into masters of a methodology and outsiders. The sermon (rather than the seminar) might be the best example of the point, since the sermon attempts to make intelligible what might otherwise remain mysterious or bewildering. Derrida's critique of Lacan makes the point about psychoanalysts' desire for mastery, and no one would say that Derrida's reading seeks to be the final word. Yet, his reading, like many others, follows a narrow stylistic groove, with its sound pitched for specially educated ears. The question concerns what it means if the reading possesses "too much subtlety."

The quotation that begins Poe's story is attributed to Seneca, but as far as scholars can tell, is not Seneca's. Also, this quotation is placed in a similar position as the purloined letter, i.e., suspended below the title, flanked by two bland columns. Dupin describes the position of the purloined letter as follows: "At length my eyes, in going the circuit of the room, fell upon a trumpery filigree card-rack of pasteboard, that hung dangling by a dirty blue ribbon, from a little brass knob just beneath the middle of the mantelpiece."[30] The epigraph, like the letter, is too obvious, too simple, something with which one would not want to dirty one's hands. Yet, "the divine mystery of life is its simplicity." Lacan and Derrida seem not only to have missed the pseudo-Seneca quotation, but also to have missed its lesson.

Most of my readers live in a critical world that celebrates indeterminacy and ambiguity, but, as Waite says, "We should never rush . . . to celebrate textual 'undecidability' or 'heteroglossia' at the cost of blinding ourselves to hegemonic overdeterminations or of making determined political actions impossible."[31] What Lacan and Derrida leave out by focusing on the world of well-plumbed intertextuality is the quotidian world of lived history and society, a world in which many people are not attuned to literary allusions and are untrained in the jargon of literary and psychoanalytic theory. The readings of Poe's text by Lacan and Derrida seem bound to a vertical vortex, and vortex here has at least two meanings: (1) a mass of whirling gas or liquid, especially when sucked spirally toward a central axis; and (2) one of the rotatory masses of cosmic matter that in the Cartesian philosophy filled all of space and from which the material universe evolved. For Derrida and Lacan, the world emerges from "the cosmic matter" of the text, rather than the text being a product of the world and its history or a call for action. In the interpretations of Poe's text by Marie Bonaparte, Lacan, Derrida, and even Barbara Johnson, little appears about the history of what goes on in the diegetic space of Poe's story, nor is space devoted to historicizing, say, by examining the history of the crime story. Also, the focus for much of the criticism is Dupin, the complex character who is learned but who is always positioned *inside* the tale. The narrator never gives the reader a description of Dupin meandering about as if in the open. He lives in a closed world of books and letters—i.e., an intertextual world. It should be noted that Dupin's world is vertical, hierarchical; a definite chain of command and power exists.

The vertical orientation of Derrida and Lacan coincides with the stance one would expect from those engaged in methodological combat. (Vertical positioning is an important part of the *Brazil* chapter, below.) By contrast, Gadamer is the speaker for the horizontal, for horizons, for a broad historical picture that includes material considerations, and is very much concerned with the pedestrian, the plebeian, or as Gadamer would call it, the *sensus communis.* One of the reasons some people often criticize hermeneuticists stems from the latter's horizontal positioning. When everyone else is off to the Critical Crusades, bashing other critics, hermeneuticists seem to be lying down, relaxed, listening. Unlike the crusades of the Middle Ages, the Critical Crusades deliberately exclude "simple" folk, though these same critics claim to be speaking on behalf of those people. Generally, critics talk to themselves. Edward Said has pointed out that new books of literary criticism reach an audience of about 3,000, composed mainly of academics, and that much of this criticism exhibits a "private-clique consciousness embodied in a kind of critical writing that has virtually abandoned any attempt at reaching a large, if not mass, audience."[32] This is why, by the end of this chapter, I want to shift the focus of attention away from Dupin toward the street, toward the outside world, toward the women and children outside Minister D—'s window, toward these "simple" people and "simple" matters, or, if you like, toward obvious matters that have been ignored.

What about the pseudo-Seneca quotation? Is it supposed to be from Seneca the Elder, or Seneca the more famous Stoic philosopher? Why does Poe attribute the quotation to Seneca? Why didn't Poe put "Anonymous" after the line, for instance? Some evidence suggests that the opening epigraph could be seen as a counterpart to the story's final quotation from Crebillon's *Atrée: "Un dessein si funeste / S'il n'est digne d'Atrée, est digne de Thyeste"* ["A design so deadly, / If not worthy of Atreus, is worthy of Thyestes"]. Seneca (4 B.C.?–A.D. 65), the son of a rhetorician, wrote a tragedy called *Thyestes.* In addition, the younger Seneca wrote the *Epistulae Morales,* 124 letters divided into 20 books, fictional letters addressed to Lucilius Iunior. The nexus with "The Purloined Letter" becomes stronger in light of two other details in Seneca's life: (1) In 41 A.D., he was banished to Corsica by Claudius on a charge of committing adultery with the emperor's niece; similar to the situation in "The Purloined Letter," Seneca was involved in an indiscretion in the royal boudoir. And (2) in 65 A.D., Seneca was accused of participating in a conspiracy to depose Nero; some said he was to succeed to the throne—that is, Seneca would have had the power of a "king," which is one of the effects of the letter in Poe's story. I am not trying to explain away this quotation, and so far, it remains an enigma, a riddle (Old English for "advice," "interpretation"), a piece of advice that remains outside the frame, for it is not at all clear that the narrator of Poe's story placed the Latin quotation at the tale's beginning, suspending it below the title. Much like the letter in Poe's text, the quotation has been "mantled," concealed, cloaked, hidden, by being somehow too present. The word "tale" is also etymologically related to enigma, to the Greek *ainos* and the verb *ainissesthai*—to speak in riddles. I am not sure why Poe put this pseudo-Seneca quotation at the beginning of the story, but pinning down authorial intention is not the point.

We can turn to another quotation, to Derrida's comments on the quotation marks around the excerpt from Crebillon's *Atrée*. I think it is important to note that Derrida transforms these quotation marks into what he calls Dupin's "signature." Of course, no "real" signature is given by Dupin, but Derrida allegorizes the text, as does Lacan. The critic speaks otherwise about the letter, the literal.

As Johnson explains, Derrida's focus on the signature becomes the locus for a personal attack on Lacan. Derrida believes that Lacan, who replaces Freud as the father figure of psychoanalysis, is somehow envious that Marie Bonaparte, who was the first to interpret Poe "psychoanalytically," received Freud's endorsement and affection in a "signed" foreword to her book, *The Life and Works of Edgar Allan Poe: A Psycho-Analytic Interpretation* (French edition, 1933). Derrida writes:

> The entire Seminar is opened by the project, repeated elsewhere a hundred times, of "taking Freud's discovery seriously" and of basing "the instruction of this Seminar" on this discovery, and to do so against the corruption which the letter of Freud has suffered in his colleagues' institution; and "what Poe's tale demonstrates through my efforts" collaborates with the return of Freud's text to its proper place. From this position the Seminar ridicules the too rapid identification of (all) the other analysts with Dupin, with a Dupin about whom they do not see that in possessing the letter he still resembles the minister, and thus finds himself in the latter's place and begins like the minister to become feminized, to become identified with the Queen. The author of the Seminar excludes himself from the analytic community. We, henceforth, are Freud, Poe, one of the two Dupins, and I. . . . [FV, 450]

There are further jibes at Lacan: "This signed attestation, from Freud's hand, must be read here. For amusement, but also in order to appreciate how the King, in effect, will have seen that in carrying off the last plume at first hand, he finds himself having mobilized many since his death, while awaiting restitution, that is, restoration. In the position of being dead too soon, *a priori,* he will have never prefaced the Seminar. . . . But one can dream of the figure a foreword by Freud would have made" [FV, 457]. One might also dream that both Derrida and Lacan express the desire to be king of France, in a sense, to gain power over the letter, over language, to expose everything, not the sort of exposure that denudes, but a display that empowers.

While Johnson diligently calls to our attention the many times Derrida deconstructs himself, his own text, she does not alert her readers to the fact that Derrida's persona, like Lacan's, switches from the plural to the *singulière*, from the "we" to an "I." In his essay as well, Derrida employs "we" (FV, 492). However, toward the end of his essay, he writes, "I have indicated only the most salient [effects] in order to begin to unlock a reading . . ." [FV, 492]. Who is this "we" in Derrida's text? And how neutral a metaphor is that of finding keys to unlock texts? In *This Sex Which Is Not One,* Irigaray says, "Female sexuality has always been conceptualized on the basis of male parameters." This argument is similar to the one Derrida makes about Lacan's reading of Poe, which indicates that Derrida is probably aware of the other ways to interpret the image of keys unlocking texts.

One of Derrida's main arguments against Lacan and psychoanalysis is that psychoanalysis sees itself everywhere. "In whatever it turns its attention to, psychoanalysis seems to recognize nothing but its own (Oedipal) schemes." The rhyme to this "nothing but" that Derrida directs at Lacan appears in his own reading of Poe's story. Derrida finds his own desires in "The Purloined Letter"; he locates the material to refute Lacan, but there is more to Poe's story than either psychoanalysis or deconstruction; there are people outside, outside Derrida's reading (as he knows), and outside Minister D—'s window. But I am getting ahead of myself.

In another sense, what Lacan and Derrida do could be seen as the sort of appropriation Gadamer talks about, that is, making a text one's own. To continue in this vein, I want to show how Poe's text could be appropriated hermeneutically as well. In light of its darkness, its surplus of meaning, "The Purloined Letter" could be used as an example of certain hermeneutical ideas, such as the objection to scientific methodologies, and of an older hermeneutical belief: that the purpose of interpretation is to put yourself, psychologically, in place of the author. (Someone might object that I am having hermeneutics see itself everywhere, which, to an extent, seems just to me, insofar as hermeneutics deals with understanding, and understanding goes on in innumerable places and situations.) Below I will show how Poe's text can be applied to hermeneutics itself to illustrate certain principles of nineteenth-century hermeneutics.

In the romantic hermeneutics of Schleiermacher and Dilthey, one of the goals of understanding was a psychological reconstruction, finding out what the author intended. From this we get Dilthey's notion of *Sichhineinfühlen,* or empathy. Along these lines, Dupin could easily be a romantic hermeneuticist, one who protests against ahistorical, noncontextual methodologies, and one who tries to get "inside" the minds of others. The Prefect could be a representative of scientific method. Poe says the Prefect "had a fashion of calling everything 'odd' that was beyond his comprehension, and thus lived amid an absolute legion of 'oddities.' " To locate the letter, the Prefect applies his methods assiduously, using microscopes, sticking needles into the bindings of Minister D—'s books, checking for cavities in the furniture where the missing missive might be hidden. When the Prefect comes up empty, he turns to Dupin, who, through dialogue, spots the difficulty immediately. Dupin explains that the Prefect's measures "were good in their kind, and well executed; their defect lay in their being inapplicable to the case, and to the man. . . . [The police] consider only their own ideas of ingenuity; and, in searching for anything hidden, advert only to the modes in which *they* would have hidden it." All that the Prefect has done, Dupin says, is but "an exaggeration of the application of one principle or set of principles of search."

To illustrate his own method of understanding through a kind of mind-meld, Dupin relates the story of the boy who plays the even-odd game, a game of guessing whether your opponent has an odd or even number of marbles in hand (a game at least as old as Book II of Cicero's *De Finibus* II.xvi.52). One schoolboy was especially good at winning the game. Dupin says that "upon inquiring of the boy by what means he effected the thorough identification in which his success consisted, I received answer as follows: 'When I wish to find out how wise, or how stupid, or how good, or how wicked is any one, or what his thoughts at the moment, I fashion the expression of my face, as accurately as possible, in accordance with the expression of his, and then wait to see what thoughts or sentiments arise in my mind or heart, as if to match or correspond with the expression'" [PL, 340].[33] In other words, the boy becomes a mirror to his opponents. He contorts himself in accordance with the look of the other. He adapts himself to the situation at hand, something a good rhetorician would do. Moreover, the boy tries to metamorphose himself into the other, to feel what his opponent feels, think what the opponent thinks: the schoolboy embodies otherness, temporarily, so that it is not so much sympathy or empathy, but a reliving, a resubjectifying. In a late text (*Plan der Fortsetzung zum Aufbau der geschichtlichen Welt in den Geisteswissenschaften* [1903–1911]), Wilhelm Dilthey writes: "The basis of the human studies is not conceptualization but total awareness of a mental state and its reconstruction based on re-living or re-experiencing [*Nacherleben*]," a kind of "living back."[34]

In the story of even-odd, the schoolboy is giving back the expression of his playmates. There is a kind of give and take, a dialogical movement to this game, and though I seem to set the rhetorical (Dupin and the schoolboy) in opposition to logic or scientific method (the Prefect), I want to overcome the usual split between rhetoric and logic by highlighting the dialectical nature of human thinking as characterized by Gadamer in *Truth and Method.*

One of the things that can happen as we read, as we engage in a dialogue with the text, is an interplay between the past and the present; this goes back to Gadamer's notion of the *Horizontverschmelzung.*[35] As I said earlier, part of this horizontal approach will call for me to look back at the history of the crime story, an attempt to historicize what has been absent in the criticism of "The Purloined Letter," at least the criticism cited in this text.

An excellent article on the history of the modern crime story and of methods used for crime detection is Carlo Ginzburg's "Clues:

Morelli, Freud, and Sherlock Holmes."[36] Ginzburg reminds us that the methods used by fictional detectives like Sherlock Holmes were not mere inventions, nor was the beginning of the detective story (an expression first used in 1878 by the American novelist Anna Katherina Greene in her book *The Leavenworth Case*) an accidental development. Ginzburg writes:

> In England from about 1720 onward, in the rest of Europe (with the Napoleonic code) a century or so later, the emergence of capitalist relations of production led to a transformation of the law, bringing it into line with new bourgeois concepts of property, and introducing a greater number of punishable offenses and punishment of more severity. Class struggle was increasingly brought within the range of criminality, and at the same time a new prison system was built up, based on longer sentences of imprisonment. But prison produces criminals. In France the number of recidivists was rising steadily after 1870, and toward the end of the century was about half of all cases brought to trial. The problem of identifying old offenders, which developed in these years, was the bridgehead of a more or less conscious project to keep a complete and general check on the whole of society. [P. 105]

Given these statistics on nineteenth-century France, it is not strange that Poe chose France as the setting for "The Purloined Letter."

Inasmuch as the Ginzburg article is mainly about Holmes and crime detection in late nineteenth-century England and its colonies, it does not readily connect up with Poe's story. However, Ernest Mandel's *Delightful Murder: A Social History of the Crime Story* will certainly prove useful here.[37] Mandel mentions the problem of recidivists and how to control them: "A real breakthrough occurred around 1840 with the invention and rapid spread of photography. Records of both criminals and clues could then be made, kept, and stored for future use. It was not long before the taking and recording of fingerprints followed. It is therefore no accident, as Walter Benjamin noted, that there is a chronological correspondence between the discovery of photography and the origin of the detective story."[38] The sort of files the authorities used permitted the systematic examination of clues. This systematizing keeps things under control—if nothing else, the files are in order. But Mandel claims that this systematizing made society, in general, less human. With the turning of evidence into a system, "all human relations in bourgeois society thus tend to become quantifiable and empirically predictable. They are broken down into components and studied as under a microscope (or through a computer) as though they were physical substances like a piece of metal or a chemical, or objective phenomena like the price fluctuations of some company's stock on the market. The analytical mind holds sway over the synthetic one. No dialectical balance between analysis and synthesis is ever even considered. And what is the mystery story if not *the apotheosis of the analytical mind* in its purest form."[39] Mandel also sees that "the real subject of the early detective stories is . . . not crime or murder but enigma."

"The Purloined Letter" is about enigma and darkness. Remember Dupin's famous statement to the narrator: "If it is any point requiring reflection, we shall examine it to better purpose in the dark" (PL, 330). As Mandel says, these early detective stories are not about crime. No one is arrested in "The Purloined Letter." The more "criminal" verb "steal" is replaced by "purloin." The story involves indiscretion, intrigue, infringement, as well as deception, but where one would expect the word "crime" to appear, one sees the word "affair" in its place—for we are talking about the lives of the rich and famous, people who can be identified merely by their initials (e.g., Minister D—). In spite of the absence of a legal crime, an exchange of capital does take place: Dupin reaps the Prefect's 50,000 francs, and the Prefect apparently does well in the deal too, because the reward offered for the return of the letter is most likely more than 50,000 francs. The exact figure is never mentioned, though the Prefect stresses that it is "a very great deal—a very liberal reward" (PL, 337). Clearly, this is an affair of the upper class, which is not subjected to the same laws and constraints as an affair involving the masses. (Mandel says that the brilliant sleuths in crime stories are usually of upper-class origins [p. 15].) It is telling that the Prefect and the police go to such lengths for a case that is not murder.

As the Prefect tells Dupin, the letter is being used for "political purposes" (PL, 333). What we have here is the politics of paper, the power of paper. Of course, money is power as well as paper, but money does not change hands when the Prefect gives Dupin the 50,000 francs: he writes Dupin a check! Politics in modern society involves the control of paper—documents, files, criminal records. A check can be traced in ways that money cannot, because another step must follow before the check can be translated into money, which can then be used in exchanges for goods. "Check" is also the Old French for "defeat." Thus, the Prefect is signaling his defeat to Dupin with the check. He has been outsmarted. Etymologically, "check" is a term from chess, indicating that the king is in danger. The contents of the letter endanger the royalty in Poe's story.

Yet, the end of the story is not a checkmate, because the king survives. What happens is more like an *en passant,* in at least two senses. In one sense, Dupin makes the *en passant* move on Minister D—, removing him from the political game, though the Minister's position is not assumed by anyone else. In another sense, Dupin uses a pawn (his employee) to pass by the window of Minister D—'s apartment and fire a musket ("without ball") into a crowd of women and children. Thus the class of people below the Minister's window are turned into pawns, too. After Dupin's employee passes, he passes himself off as "a lunatic or a drunkard" (PL, 348). During this disturbance, when Minister D— is unaware of what is going on behind his back, Dupin is free to remove the letter from its envelope and make the final exchange of paper in the story.

Even if only for a short time in the story, the worlds of the sophisticated and the simple, the arcane and the mundane, come together. The street plays a significant role, so that the pedestrians bear part of the burden of the letter exchange. One doesn't play chess without pawns, and everyone knows the importance of pawns in the endgame, the time when one can convert pawns into more powerful pieces. The royalty of pawns is not obvious, but my aim is to keep readers aware that the aristocratic and the pedestrian exist in the same world. Pawns carry this message in them through their transmutability, through their constant threat of transubstantiation, even if this threat in Poe's story remains untranslatable.

The relevance of "The Purloined Letter" lies in remembering its movement between the urbane and the rustic, in what Stanley Cavell calls "the uncanniness of the ordinary." In the essay by that name, Cavell discusses Poe's tale as an allegory for the lesson of ordinary language philosophy, a tale that seeks to awaken us to the everyday, to the domestic, when the impulse is to overlook the domestic in favor of the exotic, the extraordinary.[40]

CHAPTER TWO

$\mathcal{S}$ ocrates and Cicero, Truth-telling and Lying

Truth is a topic on which we tend to speak at cross-purposes, which is a sign that we haven't thought much about it. The subject in fact hardly ever comes up in academic literary study. I won't say the word is never used, but it does not have much status, which is another way of saying that it isn't of much use.—Gerald L. Bruns[1]

Both the poetical and philosophical types of speech share a common feature: they cannot be "false." For there is no external standard against which they can be measured and to which they might correspond. Yet they are far from arbitrary. They represent a unique kind of risk, for they can fail to live up to themselves. In both cases, this happens not because they fail to correspond to the facts, but because their word proves to be "empty."
—Hans-Georg Gadamer[2]

So truth is, in time, the absurd and fertile quest of lies, which we pay with tears and blood.—Edmond Jabès[3]

We can begin with heresy and work our way from there: Truth and falsehood are built into the language we use, so that we cannot help but lie. Now to try to say something truthful about truth and lies, thereby introducing the liar's paradox.

In short, truth bores most people, or as Bruns opines, it doesn't seem to be of much use. In the beginning of his essay, "*Was ist Wahrheit?*", Gadamer mentions the story of Pilate, who asked Jesus, "What is truth?", and then walked away.[4] This walking away compels our attention. Gadamer interprets this walking away as Pilate's belief that Jesus' notion of truth had nothing to do with the Roman state Pilate represented, even though Jesus was called the Jewish "king." While Gadamer sees Pilate's question as a question about politics and power—and I want to return to that—for the moment I prefer to concentrate on two interpretations of this story, with the second one reserved for the latter part of this chapter. The first interpretation is similar to Gadamer's, but is seemingly naive; that is, that the possible answer to his own question bores Pilate, and his disinterest manifests itself in his walking away. For the purpose of this text, I agree with George Sand, who said, "The truth is too simple: one must always get there by a complicated route." Perhaps a paraphrase would fit better here: The truth is too dull: one must always get there by an interesting route. Or perhaps: The truth is too bright, and one must not approach it straight on, since its luminosity blinds, but sideways. Think of the story of Jesus' transfiguration (Matthew 17). Or of the following Emily Dickinson poem:

Tell all the Truth but tell it slant—
Success in Circuit lies
Too bright for our inform Delight
The Truth's superb surprise

As Lightning to the Children eased
With explanation kind
The Truth must dazzle gradually
Or every man be blind—

It is as if one had to earn truth, to travel a long distance to get at it, to suffer for it, to be surprised by it, so that the shock would be called insight, a revelation. We want our truth to be memorable. Sometimes, like Pilate, we would rather walk away from a truth that is right in front of us than to learn the truth too easily. A good example of this is a story Robert Nozick includes in his *Philosophical Explanations:* "A person travels for many days to the Himalayas to seek the word of an Indian holy man meditating in an isolated cave. Tired from his journey, but eager and expectant that his quest is about to reach fulfillment, he asks the sage, 'What is the meaning of life?' After a long pause, the sage opens his eyes and says, 'Life is a fountain.' 'What do you mean, life is a fountain?' barks the questioner. 'I have just traveled thousands of miles to hear your words, and all you have to tell is that? That's ridiculous.' The sage then looks up from the floor of the cave and says, 'You mean it's not a fountain?' "[5] The truth the sage offered is too simple. One expects that any important truth will be mysterious, dark, perplexing, as if the oracular nature of truth were the payment for the effort. When the truth is simple, disappointment sets in, the kind of disappointment one feels when one finds out that the culmination of the Eleusinian Mysteries was an ear of corn cut in silence.[6]

Recall in "The Purloined Letter" that the object everyone is searching for—the letter—is in plain view on the mantelpiece. What does it mean that people cannot see what is most obvious? For one, that often we become dead to the world and need to awaken to it again and again. "The truth is too simple: one must always get there by a complicated route." That complicated route to the letter on the mantelpiece becomes the story "The Purloined Letter."

This chapter is an invitation to a labyrinth, or at least a long journey through a discussion about truth-telling and lies—back to the ancients, namely Socrates and Cicero, and then back to Gadamer's appropriation of an ancient view of language.

I

From an analytic philosopher's perspective, the following discussion of truth-telling and lies will appear ludicrous. The analytic philosopher of language produces a logical system of statements about the world: The cat is on the mat. Better yet, the philosopher substitutes symbols for words, so that one gets sentences like "It is true that p if and only if p."

What surfaces is a series of descriptions not about what an experience of truth looks like, nor what the character of a truthful human being is like, but descriptions of a methodology for proving truth and for finding facts. For instance, a speaker must know a sufficient number of facts to be able to justify asserting p. Charles Taylor calls this a designative theory of language in which one need not necessarily speak to anyone else.[7] A designative theory of language assumes that language serves to refer to things. On this view, "[Language] is an instrument of control in gaining knowledge of the world as objective process. And so it must itself be perfectly transparent; it cannot itself be the locus of mystery, that is, of anything which might be irreducible to objectivity" (p. 226). However, Taylor says that "language cannot be confined to the activity of talking about things" (p. 233). The cat might be on the mat, but where is the unicorn?

The analytic philosophers of language want to clear up mysteries and relieve language of its messiness, its worldliness. Conversely, rhetoric and hermeneutics must make their way in the streets among idioms, idiots, rascals, madmen, tricksters, lawyers, entertainers, colloquial confusions, neologisms, and foreign languages in which one's ear cannot tell an elision from a single word, nor a cat in French from a shah in Iran. The analytic philosophers want to help by establishing consistency and stability, but the stability they seek is exactly the sort the street does not provide—so they block off the street. That analytic philosophies of language will have no truck with the discourse of the streets means, for one, that everyday language is irreducible to symbolic constants, given the rapid changes in colloquial banter. These changes fall under the category of relativism, which some view as another disreputable feature of rhetoric and hermeneutics.

As Gadamer mentions in "The Hermeneutics of Suspicion," a great many people find rhetoric and hermeneutics to be less than noble. Rhetoricians, always aware of the moment, can shift with changing situations. The following passage from Cicero's defense of Cluentius, in which Cicero is responding to someone who made a charge based on earlier statements by Cicero, spells out what infuriates some about rhetoric: "The terms of my address were prompted by the demands of the moment rather than by any authoritative conclusions I might have formed. . . . As counsel for the prosecution I had to make it my first objective to work upon the emotions of the public and the judges. So I was determined to draw upon every available rumour which could supply me with criticisms of the court."[8] Who would count rumor-mongering noble? The pure of mind will distance themselves from such talk and refuse to descend to this level—i.e., street level, the concrete. The pure will keep their minds and hearts sealed off from rhetoricians like Cicero, who set out to "work" upon their emotions and to change their minds, as Cicero apparently did to Pompey. In a letter to Lentulus Spinther, Cicero writes: "I happened to be dining with Pompey that evening. It was a better moment than had ever come my way before, because we had just had our most successful day in the Senate since your departure. So I talked to him, and I could flatter myself that I led his mind away from all other notions and focused it upon upholding your position."[9] Consistency does not lie in changing your mind, nor in having your mind changed for you, so that a consistent philosopher prefers to be single-minded, self-contained, and will not let his mind be led away.[10]

Everyday language, however, behaves like the genie who keeps popping out of the bottle, refusing containment. That the genie does not remain a genie, but turns into other creatures, maddens the bottlers further. Just when they thought they had the matter under control, the tables get turned and the genie takes over. Heidegger conveys this turn of events with his famous phrase, "*Die Sprache spricht,*" for usually human beings like to think that they do the talking.

II

Truth receives far more play than its counterpart falsehood, though falsehood, in its various guises, is much more complex than a simple polarity to truth. Gadamer says that being and not-being (substitute truth and falsehood here) are fundamentally inseparable, so it seems justified to explore the ancient conception of lies and lying if only to balance the scales a bit. Given Gadamer's account of the issue, truth and non-truth rely on each other; one makes the other more distinct. This resembles the Eleatic Stranger's statement in the *Sophist* (259a): "Whenever we say 'non-being,' we do not speak of something opposite to being but only other." Perhaps the abundance of writing about truth tells us something—perhaps that truth is more common than its otherness—for it is difficult to imagine how human interaction could proceed if lies and lying predominated, a point not far from Kant's conclusion in the *Groundwork* about false promising. Lying and truth-telling must live together.

For some reason, we have color associations with truth and falsehood. Truth is pure whiteness, the kind that blinds, and lies are darkness, which leads to expressions like "white lies"—meaning, in most cases, that one's intentions were pristine when one uttered the lie, but the lie is still dark, impure. To appeal to "white lies" is to try to engage in blending. A blending of light and dark permits us to make our way through the world without stumbling.[11] Perhaps this helps explain why a truth appearing against a background of truth eludes us, the way we might miss the flight of a white butterfly in a snowstorm, odd as such an occurrence would be.

Back to heresy. Language is inherently neither true nor false, for people establish these categories after words are spoken, written, or otherwise communicated in more or less intelligible circumstances. As Aristotle puts forth in *De Anima,* "Falsity is always in composition." Such seems to be the case with truth as well: truth seems to be above the categories of operations and results.[12] Language provides a background against which truth and lies make their appearances between people, depending on our perceptions, knowledge, and understanding. As Plato insists, if our perceptions and knowledge are faulty, the foreground and background become confused, the kind of confusion Escher exploits in drawings like *Fish and Scales.*

Language allows us to speak and be heard; it provides its own acoustics. For instance, we might think of an echo as language bouncing off language. For the moment, think of language as background. Language gives us substance to talk about being and offers a background, or a form, in which nonbeing can be spoken of, and heard. Can there be a silence that lies? Can we talk about the truth or falsity of nonutterances? Of emptiness?

In the fifth chapter of his fifth book *On Architecture,* Vitruvius discusses the use and placement in theatres of bronze or earthenware "sounding vases," vessels that would take in sound and act as amplifiers. He writes, "They are to be so made that, when they are touched, they can make a sound from one to another of a fourth, a fifth and so on to the second octave. . . . The vases are to be placed there that they do not touch the wall, and have an empty space around them and above. They are to be placed upside down."[13] The emptiness of the vases, their inversion, the emptiness around the vases—all this contributes to the enhancement of a speech, a play, a *logos*. This emptiness, properly constructed, will turn sound into music. With the help of one Aristoxenus, Vitruvius provides his readers with a diagram showing how the placement of the empty vases in the theatre can result in music and give the audience pleasure. As Vitruvius explains, "The voice, spreading from the stage as from a centre and striking by its contact the hollows of the several vases, will arouse an increased clearness of sound, and, by the concord, a consonance harmonising with itself."[14] We might assume that this sound enhancement by the strategic placement of emptiness, and empty containers, will contribute to the verisimilitude of the theatrical performance.

I want to connect Vitruvius' vases and their essential emptiness, given how they are to be used, to lies and lying—more specifically, to lies and lying in a certain Platonic way, the way Plato in the *Sophist* talks about lies as "not-being." Of course, this is an odd way to talk about lies and lying, and the path quickly becomes treacherous, for one needs to keep in mind Gadamer's point that "nonbeing as a positive characteristic of entities means being different from other things; not being other things."[15] The sophist himself says, "Not-being reduces him who would refute it to such difficulties that when he attempts to refute it he is forced to contradict himself" (238d). The vases give shape to emptiness, which will work to enhance, or amplify, a voice. Similarly, the *logos*, or language itself, gives shape to nonbeing, so that nonbeing can make its appearance. The vases are not meant to do nothing by themselves; they are meant to function in relation to a being, a voice. Lies, too, are impotent alone. Lies depend on the background of truth and trust among human beings. In fact, lies take on the appearance of such truth and trust; an undetected falsehood retains its truthful appearance. In short, a lie (nonbeing) depends upon truth (being), because "what is" (language) gives "what is not" form, the way the sounding vases structure emptiness. As with empty vases in a theatre, I must be careful how I arrange matters here, even if the matters turn out to be empty ones, for emptiness has a strange way of reverberating.

This reverberation, the music the vases make, can be connected to Longus's story of Echo, who was taught by the Muses to play music.[16] Because her beauty and music made Pan envious, Pan sent a madness among the shepherds and goatherds, and they tore Echo to pieces. Yet, even when her limbs were buried, they still produced music, making imitative sounds. Echo copies original utterances. Echo is the disembodiment of mimesis. She becomes the disembodied or empty voice, a voice which has nothing to say for itself, the kind of voice we find unsettling. In some cases the echo educates, as in the cave scene with Adela Quested in E. M. Forster's *A Passage to India*. (As in the Nozick story about the Indian holy man, Adela Quested meets something important in a cave.) These echoes produce traces, the way music can. The repetition gets inside you, as it does Mrs. Moore in Forster's novel. For Mrs. Moore, "the echo [in the Marabar caves] began in some indescribable way to undermine her hold on life."[17] The Marabar caves "were notoriously like one another; indeed, in the future they were to be numbered in sequence with white paint." The caves hold some magic that eludes human control, so some mathematical formalizing—painting numbers on the caves—might put an end to their dangerously magical effects; at least that is the plan of one of the officials in the story. As the story progresses, Adela Quested wanders into one of the caves and becomes unsettled by the echoes inside. You meet yourself in the Marabar caves. In this case, Adela Quested learns about herself in the caves, and decides that she should break off her engagement. Later in the novel, she says, "I have no longer any secrets. My echo has gone. . . ."[18] She no longer perceives the echo as other, but takes it for her own, an expression of her own desires. It is important to mention here that Gadamer rarely discusses the issue of truth apart from the issue of self-knowledge, even when that self-knowledge consists of the realization that one's self is not necessarily a coherent whole. The self can partake, as in Adela Quested's case, of phenomena like echoes.

In the "Temple" section, which follows the Marabar caves episode, echoes turn into prayers. At the beginning of Part III, we find the following lines repeated four times: "Tukaram, Tukaram, / Thou art my father and mother and everybody."[19] This is echo as prayer, repetition substituting for echoes. This is prayer about oneself, for Tukaram is everyone, including the person who begins the repetition. Perhaps it is not coincidence that the story of Echo hangs together with that of Narcissus in Ovid's version.

Caves reverberate. Heidegger begins his essay "Plato's Doctrine of Truth" by retelling the "allegory of the cave" in Book VII of the *Republic*. For Heidegger, the matter of truth appears in the allegory of the cave. He suggests a plurality of possibilities for language rather than a dichotomy. Instead of the true/false split, Heidegger speaks of unconcealedness or nonforgetting (*aletheia*) on the one hand, and "enclosing, hoarding, disguising, covering-up, veiling, dissimulation" on the other.[20] Not surprisingly, Heidegger ignores the sort of truth and falsity that derive from applying formulae to language. He goes on to show that the cave itself represents the Greek concept of *aletheia:* "For what is the subterranean cave other than something also quite overt in itself, but which remains at the same time sealed over and enclosed by the rounding walls of the earth in spite of its entrance."[21] Heidegger finds truth in fiction itself, in an allegory, in a story that cannot be verified. The use of *aletheia* once again calls up the notion of truth as something that is before us, but that we do not notice. According to etymologists, *aletheia* derives from *lanthano,* "to pass unnoticed, unperceived."[22] Bruns suggests that not enough attention is paid to the question "What is the truth of literature?" In part, critics avoid the issue, because the sort of truth one finds in literature is not scientific and resists tests like verifiability. The truth of literature cannot be figured through an accumulation of facts. Literature offers a different sort of truth. For the ancients, fictions are *plasmata*—i.e., things like truth—or as Wesley Trimpi might say, fictions are probabilities that pass for history.[23]

What is *plasma?* Ben Edwin Perry has explained that *plasso* and *plasma* were used by the ancient Greeks to differentiate between history and "invention on the basis of traditional material." Perry puts it like this: "The exposure of Oedipus as a babe, his encounter with the Sphinx, his slaying of his father, and his marrying of his mother, are regarded as history; but what Oedipus says to Tieresias and other characters in the play of Sophocles . . .—all this is understood to be *plasma*."[24] We could take *plasmata* as something like plausible inventions. Fictions possess an "as-if" quality. Trimpi explains that "the argument of fiction, as of rhetoric, is *implicitly* inductive—in the mind of the writer—but *explicitly* deductive in the work produced and in its effect upon the audience. In order to appeal most strongly to the emotions, the analysis of a given situation must select its premises beforehand so that the narrative argument may appear *as if* it had required no inductive process to arrive at the premises from which deduction might begin. By not having to deal with historical particulars, a fiction can remain tacit about the selection and acceptance of its premises in order to gain the emotional concentration of a deductive synthesis."[25]

Just as moderns fret over the status and value of literature, so did the ancients, who wondered whether made-up tales were lies, inventions, or entertainments, whether storytellers conveyed knowledge or truth (e.g., Plato's *Ion*), and whether poetry corrupted or improved the soul. Generally, truth for the ancient Greeks meant *things as they are*. Possessing knowledge of things as they are puts one in the position of philosophers like Socrates. Such knowledge would make us philosophers, but "philosophy is not fully human."[26] It is not surprising that in the *Symposium*, Socrates is compared to a Silenus, a statue. We learn how he would sometimes fall into trances, oblivious to cold and lack of sleep, and how he could drink as much as he wanted and never get drunk. Possessing Socratic knowledge exacts its toll, but possessing knowledge for oneself is quite different from conveying knowledge, risking loss of self-possession, putting things into words, knowing that the words have a life of their own, regardless of our intentions.

Questions of truth-telling and lying arise from the way things make their appearance in the world, in a *logos.* "Socrates is the man for whom nothing can be put into words except the question."[27] The question becomes: How to *say* things as they are? But Socrates avoids becoming tangled in that question, because he is always asking others to say how things are, to provide definitions for things. As Socrates interprets the oracle's message, Socrates' task is to test the background that is language and to bring truth to the foreground. He decides his method for doing this should be questioning, dialectic. By its nature, a question can be neither true nor false, so Socrates can appear outside the problems of truth-telling that he presents to his interlocutors. He covers himself by appearing to be the neutral questioner, a man whose sole interest is to discover, or uncover, the truth, to question the sages of the day about what they know—or think they know. But part of this is smoke, camouflage. Clearly, Socrates prejudges many of the people he questions. In the *Gorgias,* Socrates leads Gorgias to accept Socrates' viewpoints. Socrates is not neutral. He makes distinctions, he asserts; but his assertions, in certain cases, make him invulnerable to questions of truth and falsehood. He tells Callicles, "I shall have nothing to say for myself when in court" (*Gorgias* 521e), though we know that Socrates has plenty to say in the *Apology.* Nevertheless, Socrates can be forgiven, for as Austin says, "One cannot lie or tell the truth about the future."[28] Socrates harbors opinions about rhetoric before he ever meets Gorgias, which, in a way, is necessary for dialectic to proceed. For in order to refute someone, the interlocutor must have a plan in mind, a way to bring the other interlocutor to a self-contradiction. Socrates' ability to confound people irritates many readers, for it can seem as if he aims to belittle others. However, Gadamer points us in the right direction when he says that "what is important to [Socrates] is not refutation, as such, but liberating his opponent for a shared substantive inquiry . . ." (PDE, 57).

Of course, sophists, like Gorgias, have methods too. One in particular appears in much of the literature on the sophists, including Plato's *Sophist.* This method is called *diaeresis,* the division of names. *Diaeresis* consists in taking two names and discussing their differences. One difference between a sophist and Socrates is that a sophist asks, "In what respect is x different from y?", while Socrates continually asks, "What is x?" In short, we might call *diaeresis* definition by division, a way to distinguish like from like, a process that seems endless.[29] It seems impossible to come to a definitive conclusion using *diaeresis,* for one can justifiably stop only with the unique name that has no relationship or likeness to anything else. On the other hand, Socrates pursues the timeless essence of things, and it is the dogged pursuit of a matter, the striving after, that is important.

The difficulty Socrates experiences in trying to counter rhetoric and the sophists involves a lack in language, for words do not share a one-to-one correspondence with things, which means that some skewing of a thing's essence will occur in the effort to communicate that essence in language. The *logos* necessarily distorts things, so that human beings, burdened with their own shortcomings, are at pains to distinguish between truth and falsehoods, between what Piero Pucci calls the straight and the crooked *logos.*[30] Mario Untersteiner's work on the sophists emphasizes Gorgias's insight into the tragic nature of language and knowledge. Gorgias's texts lead Untersteiner to conclude that speech cannot show truth.[31] According to Untersteiner, "The ambivalence and contradictory nature of the logoi, which can be overcome only by means of an irrational intellectual act such as deception and persuasion, create the tragedy of human existence. . . ."[32] While I am not prepared to say that Gadamer would agree with Untersteiner that speech cannot show truth, Gadamer does take a less tragic view of what happens to us in language. For instance, he says, "Even concealing talk has a substantive content, inasmuch as concealment, too, is a way of exhibiting the facts of the matter—though by exhibiting them as what they are not" (PDE, 47).

For Hesiod, the difference mentioned above between the straight and the crooked *logos* can be detected by the Muses alone; human beings must live with faulty perceptions. Gadamer addresses this point in his commentary on Plato's *Seventh Letter,* in which he underscores Plato's concern over the "weakness of the *logoi,*" the instability of language that allows single words or utterances to have multiple meanings. Unlike many modern analytic philosophers of language, and even unlike the Gorgias we see through Untersteiner, Gadamer sees the weakness of the *logoi* as a benefit in language. Gadamer writes: "An unequivocal, precise coordination of the sign world with the world of facts, i.e., the world of which we are the master with the world which we seek to master by ordering it with signs, is not language. The whole basis of language and speaking, the very thing that makes it possible, is ambiguity or 'metaphor.' "[33] Gadamer contends that this ambiguity is productive; it gives us the possibility of saying something.

As we know, the sophists come to Greece bearing the message that stable, eternal truth cannot be had by human beings, but that humans can have rhetoric. Language, like human beings themselves, is variable, circumstantial, uncertain, transient, thaumaturgical.[34] With eternal truths unavailable, all we can do, the sophists tell us, is focus on the probable. The *eikos*, the probable, constitutes the realm of rhetoric.[35] In a key essay on rhetoric, Hans Blumenberg says:

> Rhetoric has to do either with the consequences of possessing the truth or with the difficulties that result from the impossibility of attaining truth. Plato combatted the rhetoric of the Sophists by suggesting that it was based on the thesis of the impossibility of truth and that it deduced therefrom its right to pass off what people could be persuaded of as what was true. . . . The rhetorical effect is not an alternative that one can choose instead of an insight that one could *also* have, but an alternative to a definitive evidence that one *cannot* have, or cannot have yet, or at any rate cannot have here and now. . . . As long as philosophy was inclined to hold out at least the prospect of eternal truths and definitive certainties, then "consensus" as the ideal of rhetoric, and agreement subject to later revocation as the result attained by persuasion, had to seem contemptible to it. But when it was transformed into a theory of the scientific "method" of the modern age, philosophy too was not spared the renunciation on which all rhetoric is based.[36]

Blumenberg sets out in his essay to recuperate philosophy for human beings. He reminds those who still side with Socrates, and now with scientific "method," that as finite human beings, we need to take our finitude into account in our thinking about rationality.

Time influences human truth, as do circumstances. Socrates refuses to acknowledge that truth might be relative, relative to ways of determining it, and contingent upon the circumstances of its appearance.

One of the contingencies rhetoricians consider concerns the question: What does the situation call for? Aristotle devotes a large portion of his *Rhetoric* (Book II) to reflections on audience. Rhetors often find themselves in situations that call for judgments about the audience they are to address. For Socrates, truth is truth, regardless of audience. This point serves as one of the major differences between Socrates and Cicero, which will be evident shortly.

Socrates usually discusses matters with only a handful of people, since questioning and answering is practically impossible with a crowd (see PDE, 84–85). He says, "I know how to secure one man's vote, but with the many I will not even enter into discussion" (*Gorgias* 474b). Along these lines, Gorgias makes an interesting qualification when Socrates asks him whether a rhetorician will be more persuasive than a doctor regarding health. Gorgias responds, "Yes, I said so, *before a crowd*" (*Gorgias* 459b, emphasis mine). A good orator can convince a crowd that he can make legitimate remarks about doctoring, or philosophizing, or banking, any number of things. By contrast, Socrates insists on experts. Experts possess knowledge (*episteme*); crowds and orators can muster only opinions (*doxa*).

In a slightly misanthropic moment, Socrates says, "The ignorant [the rhetorician] is more convincing among the ignorant than the expert" (*Gorgias* 459b). According to Gorgias, the skillful rhetorician instills belief in the mind of the listener. According to Socrates, knowledge is superior to belief; knowledge is constant, unifying, whereas belief is volatile, atomizing. Gorgias seeks a political consensus, another kind of *doxa* which Socrates berates: "Rhetoric in my opinion is the semblance of a part of politics." And when asked by Polus whether that is good or bad, Socrates answers "bad" (*Gorgias* 463d).

Enter Cicero, arguably a philosopher like Socrates, who says, "The eloquence of orators has always been controlled by the good sense of the audience, since all who desire to win approval have regard to the goodwill of the auditors, and shape and adapt themselves completely according to this and their opinion and approval."[37] Socrates would call this an endorsement of rhetor as chameleon, and Cicero does suggest a mutability for the orator. But Cicero emphasizes the rhetor's sensitivity to the audience's reactions and to the matter at hand. He does not presuppose the superiority of the orator over the people. Thus, he speaks of "the good sense of the audience." Cicero also shuns expertise for the orator in favor of eclecticism, wide learning. "The genuine orator," Cicero says, "must have investigated and heard and read and discussed and handled and debated the whole contents of the life of mankind, inasmuch as that is the field of the orator's activity, the subject matter of his study."[38] To be inventive, the orator must be able to call on an inventory of experiences and learning in order to adapt the utterances to the audience. Thus the question for Cicero's orator becomes not "What is x?" but "What is fitting to say about x?", i.e., fitting on this occasion, before this group of listeners.

Unlike Socrates, Cicero endorses acting. The orator exploits theatricality. At times, Cicero's ideal orator would become so immersed in what he was saying that he would appear "scarcely sane."[39] If an orator had to behave like a madman in order to get the jury to convict a murderer, Cicero would make no objections. Cicero's orators adapt themselves to various public situations, while Socrates remains constant among a small circle of intellectuals.

This is a good place to return to the episode with Pilate and Jesus, and to offer a Ciceronian interpretation of the story. Pilate asks Jesus, "What is truth?" and walks away. Earlier, I attributed this walking away to Pilate's boredom with the question of truth. Yet, that interpretation omits the context in which Pilate finds himself. We might see that Pilate is not walking away, but walking toward. Pilate walks toward the crowd that awaits his decision on what is to be done with Jesus. Pilate must address a crowd that wields some power, and in this situation, it is the crowd that will determine the answer to his question. In the end, the crowd pilots the situation. The political situation Pilate finds himself in drives him to heed the crowd's demands: "Pilate tried to release him [Jesus]; but the Jews kept shouting 'If you let this man go, you are no friend to Caesar; any man who claims to be a king is defying Caesar.' When Pilate heard what they were saying, he brought Jesus out and took his seat on the tribunal. . . . Pilate said to the Jews, 'Here is your king.' They shouted, 'Away with him! Away with him! Crucify him!' 'Crucify your king?' said Pilate. 'We have no king but Caesar,' the Jews replied. Then at last, to satisfy them, he handed Jesus over to be crucified" (John 19). Pilate finds no case against Jesus, but he turns Jesus over to the crowd *to satisfy them*. Cicero might judge Pilate less harshly than many, for Pilate shows a keen awareness of his situation, for instance by appealing to the custom of releasing one prisoner at Passover—an apparent ploy to divert the crowd's concentration on Jesus.

It would be a mistake to suppose that power always rests with the crowd. Cicero, like Aristotle before him, supposes that knowing truth from falsity is one of the powers the orator holds over the audience. This also seems to be the point of the *Phaedrus*. Of course, this power is used to bring the crowd over to the orator's side. In fact, Cicero says, "There is no way in which the mind of the auditor may be aroused or soothed that I have not tried."[40] In assuming the primacy of one's cause, a good orator will divert the attention of the audience from the point at issue, or will conceal that which cannot be explained away. Though the orator employs these sometimes questionable tactics, Cicero trusts that the orator acts with regard for truth and for the health of the state. As Blumenberg proffers, "Cicero starts from the premise that one can possess the truth, and gives the art of speaking the function of beautifying the communication of this truth, making it accessible and impressive."[41]

Crowds do not always gather for truth, but often for action, which raises the classic distinction between persuasion (*peitho*) and force (*bia*). *Peitho* exhibits a many-sidedness that at least one critic has tried to sort out.[42] For example, Peitho is both goddess of love and goddess of rhetoric. The verb *peitho* means both to persuade and, in the middle voice, to obey. But to Greeks, Buxton says, all *peitho* was seductive. According to Buxton, one of the best stories to illustrate *peitho*'s opposition to *bia* is the story of Odysseus and the Sirens. Seduction can prevent the use of force, but force (the tying of Odysseus to the mast) can also prevent seduction.

Blumenberg puts the matter simply: Rhetoric is an alternative to terror. Rhetoric "substitutes verbal accomplishments for physical ones."[43] One can be "moved" by a speech though remaining still. Or we might think of something like "character assassination," in which someone is verbally "killed." In these examples, something is taken *as* something else, indicating the metaphorical power of language. In its ability to make otherness seem familiar, language makes otherness less threatening, often dissipating the compulsion to rid one's self of otherness through violent means.

Taking something as something else brings us back to the lie (*pseudos*) and lying. The lie makes its appearance as a truth, and only later is categorized as a lie. For a while, the lie carries the power of truth, takes on the role of truth. Those who make use of the *pseudos* gain a power they might not otherwise have. Lies too can be said to be a substitute for violence, since they signal an exchange of power. As Sissela Bok says, "Lies affect the distribution of power; they add to that of the liar, and diminish that of the deceived."[44] To conjure up the power of the *pseudos,* think not of Socrates or of Cicero, but of Iago.

CHAPTER THREE

Coriolanus: "Unfit for Anyone's Conversation"

This is not a play about politics, if this means political authority or conflict, say about questions of legitimate succession or divided loyalties. It is about the formation of the political, the founding of the city, about what it is that makes a rational animal fit for conversation, for civility.—Stanley Cavell[1]

His switch from being the most Roman of Romans to becoming their deadliest enemy is due precisely to the fact that he [Coriolanus] stays the same.—Bertolt Brecht[2]

Aufidius: "[Perhaps it is Coriolanus'] nature / Not to be other than one thing."—Shakespeare, *Coriolanus* IV, vii, 41–42

I

Stanley Cavell's "*Coriolanus* and Interpretations of Politics" is the most powerful current essay on *Coriolanus,* and yet Cavell says *Coriolanus* is not about politics, but about "the formation of the political." With the formation of the political, rhetoric makes its entrance. Using Cavell's essay as a base, I will explore the play's rhetorical and hermeneutical concerns, such as: how language is used to control political situations; what the play tells us about application, i.e., how *Coriolanus* spoke to the concerns of English people living in the first decade of the seventeenth century; and the roles of certainty and indeterminacy, impregnability and risk in this play.

The issue of temporality and its denial continually emerges in

Coriolanus. Hans Blumenberg writes, "Rhetoric . . . is, in regard to the temporal texture of actions, a consummate embodiment of retardation."[3] Although much has been made of the parable of the belly told by Menenius in the first act, all the critical attention goes into interpreting the parable, not into examining its purpose at that particular moment in the drama.

As *Coriolanus* unfolds, it is evident that rhetoric has already broken down. According to Blumenberg, "Rhetoric implies the renunciation of force,"[4] but the citizens have apparently lost faith in language and have taken up arms. One of the citizens wishes to review the reasons for rebellion, but almost everyone else wants an end to talk and a quick movement to action, to force. "No more talking on't; let it be done. Away / away!" (I, i, 12–13). Blocking the citizens' procession to the Capitol, Menenius asks them to speak, to make some accounting of their present state, to come to some self-understanding. "Where go you / With bats and clubs?" Menenius asks. "The matter? Speak, I pray you" (I, i, 57–59). Then, he further retards their movement *by telling a story.* The story gives the people time to reconsider their planned activities. To delay the citizens even further, Menenius allegorizes; he doubles the effect of storytelling as a stalling tactic by relating a tale that requires interpretation, one that cannot be readily understood. It is the all-at-once rashness that Menenius wants to inhibit, by speaking otherwise. Yet, the citizens are not easily taken in by his strategy. In fact, in the midst of his storytelling, one of the citizens comments, "Y'are long about it," underscoring the fact that Menenius is elongating time, killing time to prevent killing people. Using a different sort of force—the power and magic of words—Menenius tethers the crowd in place and in time by weaving a spellbinding tale. Gadamer draws attention to storytelling's ability to draw out time when he remarks that storytelling "is an intrinsically inexhaustible process that can go on indefinitely."[5]

Shakespeare maneuvers in a similar way—though I do not claim to be reading authorial intention here—by staging *Coriolanus* during a time of insurrections. By telling the story of *Coriolanus,* which can also be read as an allegory, Shakespeare keeps the people in the theatre and out of the streets in rebellion. One must not rule out a certain degree of self-interestedness on Shakespeare's part in regard to telling this particular story to keep the citizens occupied. As E. C. Pettet explains in "*Coriolanus* and the Midlands Insurrection of 1607":

> Whether he was in London at the time or—as is possible—in Stratford, Shakespeare would have had a particular interest in the 1607 disturbances. By now he was himself a substantial landowner, while Warwickshire was one of the disaffected areas. Admittedly he would have had nothing to fear from the peasants personally, for he was not himself an encloser and may even have disapproved of the practice. But as a landowner he must have been concerned with the important agrarian problem, and though (as usual) his personal attitude eludes us, we know that he was involved in the controversy over the proposed Welcombe enclosures in 1614. Further, as evidence of dearth and corn shortage, we remember that the Stratford Justices' for February 1598 had noted him as one of the chief holders of malt in the town.[6]

This, of course, puts Shakespeare in the position of the patricians in *Coriolanus* who have all the grain while the people go hungry. Yet, because Cavell has found the political readings of the play uninteresting, he barely attends to this class conflict. "A political reading is apt to become fairly predictable once you know whose side the reader is taking, that of the patricians or that of the plebeians."[7] Two comments about this quotation. First, the play is not so simple, as Cavell's readily recognizes. In an article on a performance of *Coriolanus* at the Comedie-Française in the 1933–34 season, Felicia Londre presents evidence that audiences found the play to be both pro-plebian and pro-patrician.[8] Think of the difference between Brecht and Beethoven's perspectives on Coriolanus. It seems to me that the play offers an account that can be read at least two ways, that is, both for and against Coriolanus. Second, the Cavell quotation about a predictable political reading seems to discount a dialectical approach that might come to say that whatever side one is on, both sides must exist in the same space, or city, and it is this communion among the members of a community that is at stake. Certainly the citizens listening to Menenius's parable know which side he is on, and their reasons for listening deserve our attention. For Cavell, this getting along is based in language. Language is where he takes up his political position; it is the locus on which he confers power. Yet, this orientation excludes a large, raw portion of the drama that always threatens to shut down language (and at the same time compels the use of language): the threat of physical violence. Cavell fails to address this threat, for it is the ugly underbelly of the play that is uncivilized, the very thing Menenius wants to avoid. Even though Cavell speaks of anality (e.g., the pun on the last two syllables of the main character's name) and desire, he does not shake out both ends of the question of power. For, power comes not only through eloquence or simply storytelling. It also comes through the end of a gun barrel or at the point of a sword. The latter is the kind of power that motivates Menenius's speech, according to Brecht—the power of death. *Coriolanus* calls our attention to the dialectics of death, its ability to end discourse and, at the same time, motivate discourse.

Shakespeare makes Coriolanus the ugliness spoken of above, for Coriolanus becomes death for the people of Corioli—the blood of the men of Corioli covers Coriolanus after the battle. Volumnia says, "Before him he carries noise, and behind him he leaves tears. / Death, that dark spirit, in's nervy arm doth lie, / Which, being advanced, declines, and then men die" (II, i, 164–67). Also, Coriolanus represents a threat to language itself by his unwillingness to speak, to partake of conversation. Unlike Menenius, who continually tries to retard anxious groups by twice saying, "One word more" (III, i, 214–15 and 309), in order to make a space for rhetoric, Coriolanus prefers actions to words: "Let deeds express / What's like to be their words" (III, i, 133–34). What is it Coriolanus dislikes about words? The nature of words opposes his nature.

In the mouths of all, except Coriolanus, words mutate, change. Words go this way and that, depending on circumstances, and this irks Coriolanus: "Trust ye? / With every minute you [the citizens] do change a mind, / And call him noble that was now your hate, / Him vile that was your garland" (I, i, 181–85). Coriolanus seems ignorant to the reasons opinions change like the winds, which leads him to say, "I banish you [the people]. / And here remain with your uncertainty!" (III, iii, 123–24). Rhetoric, and discourse in general, deal in probabilities, not certainties, but Coriolanus valorizes certitude. He refuses to subject himself to contingencies and to time-bound customs. For instance, when the senators advise Coriolanus that he needs to ask for the people's voices, he responds, "I do beseech you / Let me o'erleap that custom" (II, ii, 137–38). In fact, Coriolanus frightens simply because he is a man of his word; that is, he is *always* a man of his word. Temporality, probability, mutability—all these belong to rhetoric. Coriolanus is antirhetoric. He is absolute, independent (except as far as he listens to Volumnia), like a mathematical formula. Naturally, many people in the play note this trait of constancy. Aufidius says of him, "Yet his nature / In that's no changeling" (IV, vii, 10–11). Volumnia tells Coriolanus, "You are too absolute" (III, ii, 40). And Coriolanus himself says, "I am constant" (I, i, 240). In effect, he removes himself from time and circumstance, makes himself immune to contamination by contingencies and by communication. He banishes himself from history and from the human condition, a highly unstable condition.

Coriolanus is a character who refuses characterization. In other words, he does not want others to speak about him, if only because there is a danger that what gets said could change. Coriolanus insists on being "author of himself" (V, iii, 36), though this author forgets that to be an author one must use words over and over again with full awareness of the weakness of the logoi. Yet, we know how Coriolanus despises weakness of any sort. He will not acknowledge that character, and maybe even fate, depend in large part on what people *say* about you, so the wise thing to do is to try to influence what others say about you through persuasion. Gerald Bruns sums up this point well: "It is never enough to be a good and just man, you must be able to persuade people that *that* is exactly what you are. Fail of this persuasion and the worst consequences follow."[9] And the worst consequences do follow for Coriolanus, who cannot understand why he is misunderstood. He does not realize that understanding involves persuasion, working things out between people in conversation, in dialogue. At least one opportunity arises for Coriolanus to persuade people that he is a good and just man: when he has a chance to become consul by gaining the people's voices, which involves talking with others about who he is, or rather the person he wants them to see, which is slightly different from who he is. To become consul means taking on a different character from Coriolanus the warrior. In effect, the senators ask Coriolanus to present a different version of himself to the citizens. By now we know that Coriolanus denies versions. His condition seems to resemble that of Socrates, who in the *Apology* and the *Symposium* is always the same. Coriolanus is who he is through and through. All twenty-seven gashes in his body show the same thing, and he wants the wounds to *speak for themselves,* rather than have the people speak for the wounds, or about them. Nevertheless, the wounds speak for Coriolanus the warrior and say little about his abilities or qualifications as consul—if being consul means representing the people, being something different from a warrior. He frequently demonstrates that he sees no reason why there should be a difference between Coriolanus the warrior and Coriolanus the consul.

To return to Cavell's comments about his lack of interest in a political reading of the play, I believe that the play provides the political dialectic Cavell bypasses. Yes, Coriolanus takes sides. He stays on his own side and will not cross over, nor risk opening himself to others, which often means risking opening himself to others' interpretations of him, and to that which he reveals. Even the wounds Coriolanus seems prepared to display show themselves not to be openings, for Coriolanus believes himself to have no opening. He is the One among the Many. He presents himself as an absolute, unconditional, nonrelational, eternal whole.

II

Back to the beginning, when Menenius tells the people the parable of the belly. Cavell says, "The first mystery of the play is that this seems to work, that the words stop the citizens, that they stop to listen. . . ."[10] The citizens put aside their immediate concerns—stemming from hunger—for some greater good, the health of the city. As Gadamer points out in *Truth and Method,* listening is often more important than speaking. By stopping and attending to Menenius's story, the citizens show themselves to be human; they demonstrate a willingness to be persuaded, the first step in the formation of the political. By listening, and by applying the story Menenius tells them, the people exhibit their fitness for conversation. They are willing to be changed by the logos instead of by force.

After hearing the parable of the belly, the first citizen asks, "How apply you this?" (I, i, 148). Here the citizens transform the parable from a stalling tactic to a thing with meaning that is trying to speak to their situation. To be a partner in a conversation means to perceive that what is being said involves you. Perhaps to be political means to take all stories as stories about your own experience as well as the storyteller's. Out of this comes community and an understanding of shared experience. The sort of listening we witness in the citizens connects up with interpretation. "How apply you this?" is another way of asking how to interpret the story, and not just any interpretation will do. The citizens want an interpretation that makes them part of the story. The many are willing to be absorbed into the whole story in order to be implicated in the whole story. The people manifest a certain permeability. After all, *Coriolanus* is partly the story of a body, a body continually in danger of being dismembered.

And then we have the impermeable Coriolanus. Throughout most of the play, Coriolanus remains single-minded, fortified against attempts at persuasion. By his actions, he makes the story, but he does not want to be *part* of the story of Rome. Coriolanus reverses the expression about one who is all talk and no action. To be persuaded means to be affected, taken in, absorbed. Perhaps the tragedy of *Coriolanus* turns out to be the consequences of being persuaded, one of which is a giving up of oneself. At the moment Coriolanus allows himself to be dissuaded by his mother from destroying Rome, he recognizes that he has returned to time, to the dangers faced by human beings who listen: "Most dangerously you have with him prevailed, / If not most mortal to him. But let it come" (V, iii, 188–89). It is interesting that Coriolanus speaks of himself in the third person here, distancing himself from himself, able finally to recognize the otherness in himself, and at the same time acknowledging his mortality, admitting that his lot is the same as that of other human beings. Gadamer says that "in every expression of art, something is revealed, is known, is recognized. There is always a disturbing quality to this recognition, an amazement amounting almost to horror, that such things can befall human beings. . . ."[11] Just as Coriolanus's son dismembers a butterfly earlier in the play, Coriolanus, whom Menenius compares to a butterfly shortly after (V, iv, 11–14), is dismembered by the Volscians. In fact, Coriolanus encourages the Volscians to dismember him: "Cut me to pieces, Volsces, men and lads, / Stain all your edges on me" (V, vi, 112–13). This speech shows once again that he is willing his own dismemberment, which includes dismemberment from the body politic.

Retarding time helps us to live and keeps us, at least temporarily, from violent ends. In certain ways, the beginning of *Coriolanus* mirrors its ending. In the first act, Menenius is able to stop the citizens from acting hastily by employing the *logos,* telling a story. In the last act, when the story is about to end, Menenius the storyteller is absent. No one is around to tell a story, to elongate time, so that a rash, violent act might be put off. During the quarrel between Aufidius and Coriolanus before the lords of Corioli, the lords try to stop matters with speech. "Peace, both, and hear me speak," says one of the lords (V, vi, 111), and when the people of Corioli call out for Coriolanus's dismemberment, another lord says, "Peace, ho! no outrage, peace!" (V, vi, 124). Finally, when it is too late, all the lords call out to retard the violence: "Hold, hold, hold, hold!" (V, vi, 131). But no one is around to tell a story.

Cavell notes, "Exactly the power of Brecht's discussion can be said to be its success in getting us *not* to interpret, not, above all, to interpret food, but to stay with the opening fact of the play, the fact that the citizens of Rome are in revolt because there is a famine."[12] The opening fact of this play slips into forgetfulness, and by the end of the play the famine seems a distant, even minor concern. Instead of a play about confronting political issues, the play becomes a record of machinations to avoid political disasters or embarrassments of one sort or another—whether beseeching Coriolanus to present himself to the people in the manner that will gain their voices and not send them into revolt again, or attempting to prevent Coriolanus from sacking Rome after he has been banished. Overall, the play maps out a politics of avoidance. The fact that Martius enters Corioli to fight *alone* tells much about the climate and attitudes at work in this play.

While everyone else plots, plans, and delays, Coriolanus takes the straightforward approach, colliding with matters head on. For instance, when the Romans banish Coriolanus, he goes to meet Aufidius and crashes a party at Aufidius's house (IV, v). Coriolanus pledges himself to self-evidence, and encounters the same sort of difficulties analytic philosophers do when they try to deal with language in the manner of "*p* if and only if *p*." When he appears uninvited at Aufidius's feast, Coriolanus cannot understand why he is not recognized, nor can he comprehend why the people do not give their voices simply on the basis of his conduct in battle. Why talk if the evidence speaks for itself? From Coriolanus's perspective, his presentation of himself should say all that needs to be said, but he fails to take into account that darkness is at work. Coriolanus presents himself plainly enough, but that presentation enters a context that is dark with overlying interpretations of shadowy schemes and plots unbeknown to Coriolanus. Brian Vickers paints the chiaroscuro pattern of the scene:

> Shakespeare makes a brilliantly sustained exploration of drama's ability to mount separate presentation. Individual units of actions presented onstage are experienced by some characters but not by others. We, the privileged spectators, see every stage in every group's preparations, but Coriolanus sees none of them. Once he has left the battlefield, where action is *immediate and significant on its own terms* [my emphasis], he enters a political arena in which every action that reaches him has been planned, rehearsed, set up entirely in terms of the effect it will have on his role or behaviour. He does not see his mother exulting over his

bloody deeds, (I, iii), nor Volumnia and Menenius computing his wounds (II, i); he does not hear the comments and evaluations made of him by the citizens (I, i), by the two officers laying cushions in the Capitol, by the patricians in his temporary absence (III, i), by Aufidius (I, x; IV, vii). So much of the action of the play *goes on behind Coriolanus' back* . . . that it is no wonder if he seems completely puzzled by it all, unprepared to cope with what people say and do to him.[13]

Coriolanus shows himself to be unfit for conversation in a way somewhat different from that described by Cavell. Cavell says, "Although I shall come to agree with Plutarch . . . that Coriolanus is 'altogether unfit for any man's conversation,' I am in effect taking this to mean not that he speaks in anger and contempt (anger and contempt are not unjustifiable) but that whereas under certain circumstances he can express satisfaction, he cannot express desire and to this extent cannot speak at all. . . ."[14] While I agree with Cavell, he displaces the notion of conversation in order to substitute desire. My point is to show Coriolanus's narrow view of conversation, in contrast to one that believes conversation is a discussion between two or more people, and that conversation goes on in the same geographical and temporal space. Coriolanus enters a conversation, but any conversation he enters is a worldly, historical one that exceeds the geographical and temporal space in which he exists. For example, Coriolanus enters a conversation about the tradition of politics in Rome. The people of Rome have worked out a ritual for the election of tribunes, and Coriolanus balks at this custom of asking for voices. He enters a conversation about what it means to be a hero, a conversation that stretches back to Homer and Gilgamesh. We might call these examples part of the conversation that is tradition; it is Coriolanus's blindness to that tradition that is part of the tragedy here. Everyone except Coriolanus seems to realize that the tradition of politics includes subterfuge, shadowy activities, things that go on behind people's backs. If you are Coriolanus and continually meeting matters head on, you don't see what is going on behind you—and what is behind you and beside you is history. Furthermore, Coriolanus demonstrates no regard for what goes on behind him. He practices a politics of self-evidence.

III

In this final section, I will consider two points: (1) What it means that *Coriolanus* is not a story of a king, and how this relates to *Coriolanus* as part of a conversation about representations of authority; and (2) How Coriolanus connects up with Rome as a city.

James Holstun remarks, "Coriolanus seems the closest thing in the play to a natural-born king, but there is no room in Rome for a monarchy: Coriolanus is to be elevated no higher than a consul's seat, for the complementary republican political forces of the noble senate and the plebian tribunate will tolerate no throne."[15] In contrast to *Lear,* political stability in *Coriolanus* rests in a composite of forces rather than in a monarch. Robert Weimann connects the representation of variegated authority in Elizabethan theatre to the widening of authority brought on by the Reformation, particularly in the figure of Luther, who claims that biblical interpretation need not be legitimated by a church-appointed interpreter. Weimann writes:

> Historically speaking, the forms of representation become more complex and contradictory to the degree that the modes of authorization reconstitute themselves in reference to that more broadly national and mobile type of society which allows for much greater conflict and diversity in representational action. This new situation may roughly be characterized by saying that the traditional, preordained forms of intellectual and juridical appropriation as linked to the limited repertoire of choices in late medieval allegory or the early Tudor interlude, are superseded by more highly contingent, empirical, and experimental norms of writing, reading, and understanding. These norms presuppose a greater amount of uncontrolled or self-determined historical activity in the production and authorization, publication or performance, and reception of literary texts.[16]

In light of this, Coriolanus's comment that he is author of himself reads differently. Self-legitimation finds itself in a precarious position in a society that confers legitimation by consensus—*bia* (Coriolanus) must give way to *peitho*. Shakespeare authors Coriolanus, and represents him as someone who is supposed to be representative, not an autonomous political force. Instead of Coriolanus, it is the audience that witnesses the interplay of these forces, the consequences and responsibilities of shared authority. As Weimann says, "Rather than attempting to isolate mutually exclusive ways and means of authority in differing types of discourse, the [Elizabethan] dramatist tends to represent their entanglements and contradictions, the way authority abuses some and is used or abused by others."[17]

As I said earlier, the play can be read now as being in sympathy with Coriolanus, insofar as he is abused by a public reacting to volatile circumstances; and now again as an admonition about monological and egomaniacal force. The dispersion of power, the absence of a monarch in the play, open up new possibilities for exercising power, and for the vacillation of power. Note how the women in the play, particularly Volumnia, although lacking public positions of power, exert great influence behind the scenes. Power relations run deeper and wider than the public structures fashioned to house power.

For the city to survive, it must be able to absorb competing forces and blend them, convert them, turn opposing monologues into a heteroglossia. *Coriolanus* tells us not so much the story of Coriolanus but the story of a city—as Cavell says, "the founding of a city." Here much can be learned from Bruns's essay "Cain: Or, the Metaphorical Construction of Cities" in which we read: "The city is where power is to be found, but it does not exactly lie in the streets waiting to be picked up. . . . It works not by mechanical force but by capillary action. Power is not just domination. It operates between the extremes of *bia* and *logos,* violence and consent. It is action upon the action of others and is more labyrinthine than institutional."[18] The rhetorician finds himself at home in the labyrinth, which is why Menenius and Volumnia do not follow Coriolanus into exile, even though one is Coriolanus's surrogate father and the other his mother. To win people over, to win them back (even out of exile)— sometimes behind their backs—these are the activities of rhetoricians. A rhetorician in exile is no rhetorician, for rhetoricians require the presence of others. Yes, rhetoricians have a history of being nomads, but they always seem to turn up in cities.

$\mathcal{R}$hetoric in Milton's
Of Education

Their [Renaissance humanists] orientation was toward rhetoric rather than logic, ethics rather than metaphysics; their interest lay in questions of metaphysics rather than of epistemology.—Hanna Gray[1]

From the middle of the sixteenth century in England, [there] is a system of communication in which ambiguity becomes a creative and necessary instrument, a social and cultural force of considerable consequence. On the one hand writers complain constantly that their work is subject to unauthorized or unjust interpretation; on the other they gradually developed codes of communication, partly to protect themselves from hostile and hence dangerous readings of their work, partly in order to be able to say what they had to publicly without directly provoking or confronting the authorities.—Annabel Patterson[2]

Milton's belief [was] that oratory can accomplish more than a sceptre of a king or the sword of a warrior. . . .—Joseph A. Wittreich, Jr.[3]

The last chapter could be read as one about Rome's education—how rhetoric, in a way, saves Rome. It would miss the mark to say that *Coriolanus* is about Coriolanus's education, for he does not learn from his banishment; he does not achieve an epiphany in exile. Instead, he becomes further resolved to exact revenge. One purpose in juxtaposing these two chapters on *Coriolanus* and on Milton's *Of Education* is to appropriate the two texts as examples of opposing tendencies, one antirhetorical and the other not. Milton and his *Of Education* act as an antidote to Coriolanus, and *Of Education* outlines a program of instruction for warrior-rhetoricians—that is, soldiers who must also function as public figures when there is no war.[4]

Coriolanus appears to know nothing except war, or at least seems ignorant of what appropriate behavior looks like outside of battle. The prominence of war in both *Coriolanus* and *Of Education* reflects events in seventeenth-century England. With the Thirty Years' War, the English Revolution, and other battles, living in seventeenth-century England meant, for the most part, trying to live through war. Though Milton's attention to preparing students for war in *Of Education* appears crass and inhumane to present sensibilities, he was merely addressing the reality of his time, a time not only of continual warfare but also of censorship and the Star Chamber. According to Milton, students preparing to become England's leaders must be good warriors as well as good rhetoricians—something along the lines of Shakespeare's Henry V. It helps to remember that this prejudice was not new, since Aristotle in his *Politics* (VII, 8) also stated that a man should be capable of both business and war. In other words, Milton's tractate attempts to deal with practical problems of contemporary life. As evidence that war was a concern for Renaissance education writers other than Milton, we can turn to the last chapter of Erasmus's *The Education of a Christian Prince* (1516), which is titled "On Beginning War." There Erasmus writes, "A good prince should never go to war at all unless, after trying every other means, he cannot possibly avoid it."[5]

Published anonymously about June 4 or 5, 1644, Milton's tractate set out "the principles upon which boys should be educated for leadership in the state."[6] It is addressed to Samuel Hartlib (c. 1600–1662), a non-Englishman born in Elbing, Prussia, who was educated at Cambridge and later returned to England to become what one scholar has called the central figure in an educational renaissance in England.[7] "For the first time in English history, concentrated efforts were made to outline detailed models of a state-controlled, comprehensive educational system. Parliament was now expected to play a dominant role in educational policy, a function which it had previously not had the opportunity to exercise. To their disappointment, the planners could not overcome the inertia of Parliament, although for thirty years Hartlib was tireless in his efforts to promote their designs."[8] The Hartlib circle, which included John Dury and John Amos Comenius, thought of educating students in the same way one grows plants. "[The Hartlib's circle's] members were intimately involved in proposals for the reform of both morals and agriculture."[9] Yet, the metaphor that connected education and horticulture is not present in *Of Education*. In fact, "Milton was one of the few Renaissance writers on education to stress the importance of differences among students."[10] Agriculture, however, is not completely left out of Milton's pedagogical plans; in his tractate, Milton urges students to learn about agriculture and take part in tilling the land.

Admittedly, in spite of its agrarian considerations, Milton's education program could be called elitist, since the students Milton speaks of were to be masters, i.e., leaders of England. Ernest Sirluck puts it this way: "The education scheme of 1644 shows no interest in the intervention of the state, or in the participation of boys of the lower classes, or of girls of any class."[11] On the other hand, Hartlib and his group sought reforms for universal education, though even their plans were stratified. The Hartlib group proposed to have " 'common schools' serving the general populace, 'mechanical schools' teaching crafts to a minority, according to local needs; finally 'noble schools' to educate the upper classes. . . ."[12] Milton devotes his tractate to the formation of "noble" academies.

Charges of elitism against Milton should be qualified, however, especially since they tend to be sweeping, hyperbolic, and poorly substantiated. In addition, they occasionally reflect a superior moral attitude, as if the present were closer to the imagined pedagogical utopia. For instance, Herman Rapaport's *Milton and the Postmodern,* which seeks to bring Milton into poststructuralist discourse, typifies the reactionary nature of those who label Milton an elitist. Rapaport writes, "Like Marx, Engels, Lenin, and Mao Zedong, who had profound mistrust of the people as a whole, Milton had little respect for the mass."[13] Later, Milton's name appears in the same sentence with Himmler's. Rapaport goes on: "The famous *Defence of the People of England* was written in Latin, not English, and its prose style is utterly classical in its parodies and mimicries of every well-known Roman orator who had anything to say about politics. The *Defence* is nothing less than a scholarly and elitist tract. . . ."[14]

Although such attention-seeking prose could be ignored, one should explore these claims to illuminate the context in which Milton wrote. The fact that Milton wrote a tractate to improve education, and that he supported a plan to distribute state funds to provide a national system of elementary schools and libraries, should indicate at the very least a concern for the general betterment of the masses. Rapaport might turn to Milton's pamphlet *Considerations Touching the Likeliest Means to Remove Hirelings* for evidence of Milton's interest in educational reforms for those unable to attend the academies described in *Of Education*. And the charge that Milton was an elitist because he wrote in Latin needs to be rethought in the light of empirical evidence as well as scholarship on the important issue of literacy in seventeenth-century England. Elizabeth Eisenstein has some pertinent remarks regarding the use of Latin during this period: "Divisions between Latin and vernacular reading publics are also much more difficult to correlate with social status than many accounts suggest. It is true that the sixteenth-century physician who used Latin was regarded as superior to the surgeon who did not, but also true that neither man was likely to belong to the highest estates of the realm. Insofar as the vernacular translation movement was aimed at readers who were unlearned in Latin, it was often designed to appeal to pages as well as apprentices, to landed gentry, cavaliers and courtiers as well as to shopkeepers and clerks."[15] In fact, the teaching of Latin was common, which is why both Hartlib's group and Milton tried to make its instruction more efficient and less painful for the students. "We do amisse," writes Milton, "to spend seven or eight yeers meerly in scraping together so much miserable Latin, and Greek, as might be learnt otherwise easily and delightfully in one yeer."[16]

Although Latin training was common in the schools, this is not to say that most people in England would have been familiar with Latin. Actually, given the literacy rate in seventeenth-century England, it would be just as facile for someone to say that anyone who wrote anything in England at that time was an elitist. Lawrence Stone estimates that by 1675, the national literacy rate for men was probably hovering around 40 percent.[17] Nevertheless, the push for educational reform in the seventeenth century led to profound improvements. Stone writes: "If it is accepted that over half the male population of London was literate, that a high proportion of the one-third of adult males who could sign their names in the home counties could read, and that 2½% of the annual male seventeen-year-old-age-group was going on to higher education, then the English in 1640 were infinitely better educated than they had been before. It was a quantitative change of such magnitude that it can only be described as revolution. . . . It may well be that early seventeenth-century England was at all levels the most literate society the world had ever known."[18] To further emphasize how startling this improvement was, Stone notes that "in 1931 male university entrants [in England] formed 2.3% of the age group, which is about the same percentage as that achieved 300 years earlier."[19] Given this information, sketchy as some of it is, one ought to be wary of looking back at seventeenth-century England and imagining oneself far beyond in development.

What is the role of rhetoric in Milton's *Of Education?* Consider not how Milton uses rhetorical devices in this tractate, but what part rhetoric plays in his pedagogical proposal, in his thinking. Furthermore, how does Milton view rhetoric in his own life and as it goes on in the world—that is, as a historical, temporal matter instead of an ahistorical, theoretical concern?

Unlike today, the Renaissance was a time when people were engrossed in the history of things, in the appropriation of tradition. Before and during Milton's time, the fascination with antiquity and its texts led to a restitution of classical rhetoric, a new concern for the debate between philosophy and rhetoric which can be traced back to Plato's *Gorgias*. In fact, many proposals in Milton's *Of Education* resemble the pedagogical practices of antiquity:[20] the ancients concerned themselves with forming noble warriors and excellent citizens (some scholars attempt to associate the first concern with Sparta, the latter with Athens); they emphasized memory, and encouraged the practice of oratory in varying situations before different audiences. One of the odd things about Milton's tractate is that, in many ways, it does not seem rooted in the seventeenth century; that is, the content would seem appropriate for an educational tractate written almost any time before, say, the nineteenth century.

What is Milton's notion of a proper education? He says, "A compleate and generous Education [is] that which fits a man to perform justly, skillfully and magnanimously all the offices both private and publike of peace and war."[21] Milton sought to shape a human being who would be wise, practical, eloquent, persuasive, skilled in military and political affairs, disciplined, and exemplary— in short, an ideal orator, or rhetorician. The emphasis should be put on *ideal* here, and Sirluck does just this in his notes to *Of Education,* underlining the Platonic meaning of idea. Given that many learned people in the Renaissance considered Cicero to be an outstanding orator as well as one of antiquity's prominent models (consider the continued use of the *Rhetorica Ad Herrenium* even after it had been determined that Cicero was not the author), it is not surprising that "Milton follows the Ciceronian conception of the rigorous, broad education needed by the ideal orator."[22] Certainly, Milton's curriculum is broad, ranging from agriculture, meteorology, mineralogy, botany, and biology to logic, rhetoric, and poetics. We might call it a Cornucopia Curriculum, thereby introducing the term *copia,* to which I will return in a moment.

What the ancients desired, and what Milton seeks, is the coupling of wisdom and eloquence in a student, for eloquence without knowledge is sophistry, only pretty talk, an egregious display of mechanical skill devoid of substance, truth, or ethical concern. In the *Gorgias,* Socrates accuses the title character of sophistry. He claims that Gorgias speaks only to please and to entertain the crowd, that he concentrates almost exclusively on style, on artificial and symmetrical sentence structure to give the impression of meter, thus turning rhetoric into "cookery." It is not enough to speak well, for with practice, anyone could incorporate synecdoche, enthymemes, paramoiosis, examples, and maxims into a splendid speech on how to extract sunlight from cucumbers. But such an orator, though entertaining, would be far from the ancients' or Milton's ideal. In Milton's eyes, before one utters a syllable or prepares to compose, one must be filled with knowledge—thus, the extensive reading list in *Of Education*. Milton thinks it fruitless to force "the empty wits of children to compose Theams, verses, and Orations, which are the acts of ripest judgement and finall work of a head fill'd by long reading, and observing, with elegant maxims, and copious invention."[23]

An orator establishes credibility by being knowledgeable. One's subject takes precedence over one's style. If the matter is of great importance, the matter itself will inspire one to speak in the grand style. A good, persuasive orator is filled with learning and copiousness; and copiousness and eloquence go hand in hand. As Terence Cave points out, "*Copia* alone is a ubiquitous synonym for eloquence . . . ; it suggests a rich, many-faceted discourse springing from a fertile mind and powerfully affecting its recipient."[24] Though the matter takes priority over style, the orator must remember his audience and adapt to it, for the orator does not speak in a vacuum, nor in an artificial environment, such as the one arranged for Milton's oratorical exercises at Cambridge. In classical rhetoric, the rule is that one speaks to the occasion; the orator masters the situation. "*Copia* implies the notion of mastery, whether social or linguistic."[25]

This brings us to the association of rhetoric and power, for the inside of a cornucopia is dark and twisted. A rhetorician is someone who creates a magical effect over people, like Cipolla in Thomas Mann's "*Mario und der Zauberer*." We need only recall the names Gorgias, Protagoras, Isocrates, Demosthenes, Cicero—all influential men in their time, men whose fame can be tied to their rhetorical prowess. For the dark and twisted side of this issue, we need only recall the names Hitler and Mussolini—influential men in their time, whose infamy can be tied, in part, to their rhetorical prowess. Milton obviously recognized this link between rhetoric and power, because the students in his academy who are to learn rhetoric are also marked to become the leaders of England. Milton combines the educational goals of both Sparta and Athens by insisting that his students not only be good orators but also good soldiers, skilled in "embattailing, marching, encamping, fortifying, besieging and battering, with all the helps of ancient and modern strategems, Tactiks and warlike maxims, they may as it were out of long warre come forth renowned and perfect Commanders in the service of their country."[26] That is, Milton's students would be prepared both to use rhetoric and for its possible breakdown, which might lead to violence. A graduate of Milton's academy would be like Shakespeare's Henry V, a man who could wield words as well as a sword. Perhaps more accurately, a graduate would resemble Henry V with a touch of Machiavelli.

Since only a few youths would attend Milton's schools (about 150 in each academy), and if, as Milton planned, they were to lead all of England, they would have to possess the rhetorical and military means to gain and retain power. If this sounds Machiavellian, it is. In the *Art of War* (1521), Machiavelli urges that military leaders be trained in oratory. "An excellent general," according to Machiavelli, "is usually an orator because, unless he knows how to speak to the whole army, he will have difficulty doing anything good."[27] In the previous chapter, I showed that the formation of the political depends on listening as well as on speaking. Machiavelli makes a similar comment regarding the formation of the military: "Any prince of a republic intending to set up a new military establishment and bring reputation to such an army must accustom its soldiers to hearing their generals speak, and must accustom its generals to speak skilfully."[28] Interestingly enough, Machiavelli wants to muster an army of Cains, tillers of the soil, people who know what to do in cities: "The countrymen who are used to tilling the soil are more valuable than any others, because of all occupations, this is most used in armies."[29]

Just as the ancients noticed that rhetoric and politics are like Siamese twins, joined at vital organs, so did Milton and other Renaissance humanists. For instance, Venice, weak in many areas, tried to develop its rhetorical strength to achieve political gains. "To provide the land power she could not provide for herself and, later, to provide a tool which could help sustain the difficult role of neutral among powerful, warring clients, Venice turned toward developing a strong and skillful diplomatic corps especially trained to forge alliances."[30] Rhetoric was the core of diplomatic training. Similarly, "rhetoric is claimed as the political instrument *par excellence* by Brunetto Latini and the masters of the *ars dictaminis* as well as the great Humanist chancellors singled out by Pius II—Salutati, Bruni, Marsuppini, Poggio."[31] The rise of programmatic political uses of rhetoric can be seen as a product of the Renaissance's stress on Ciceronian oratory. Why this interest in rhetoric by states and governments? According to Brian Vickers, "The practice of rhetoric was thought to be conducive to the maintenance of order and degree."[32] A rhetorician can bring about solidarity in politically unstable times.

By including rhetoric in his curriculum, Milton would increase the chances that he would be better appreciated, his techniques more intelligible. An audience trained in rhetoric is sensitive to slippery arguments, to embellishment and allusion, and so is more likely to be attentive, to be admiring. Yet, the attention of the masses did not seem to appeal to Milton: "I seek not to seduce the simple and illiterate; my effort is to find out the choicest and learnedest."[33] (We must not forget that seduction can be a synonym for rhetoric.) It is doubtful, for instance, that Milton hoped for a large audience for his reply to Salmasius's *Defensio Regia*. Milton used rhetoric to try to influence those in power, and in so doing, increase his own standing and that of the government he represented. As Milton saw it, part of his duty included writing in order to legitimate an England without a king.

What if someone could gain complete political control, total power? Would words be necessary? Certitude cripples creativity and endorses silence. Perhaps this would help explain why many readers find God's speeches in *Paradise Lost* and Christ's words in *Paradise Regained* dull. Since God is omnipotent, rhetorical power or military power mean nothing. Omnipotence speaks for itself, guarantees stability. God cannot be defeated, which is why, unlike Milton, God does not propose an academy to train his angels in rhetoric and combat. In addition, whereas Milton admires eloquence, eloquence is the very thing Christ rejects when Satan offers it in *Paradise Regained*. Eloquence is for ambitious people, not gods. Satan is ambition incarnate, a being who depends on rhetoric for his survival. In *Paradise Lost,* Satan conquers the world not by martial force but by verbal persuasion. "In the crucial battles the antagonists contend not with weapons, but with rhetorical arguments."[34] Comus, too, is like Satan in his use of beguiling language, as is Belial.

Naturally, Milton recognized early that rhetoric could be dangerous: "Rhetoric so ensnares men's minds and so sweetly lures them with her chains that at one moment she can move them to pity, at another she can drive them to hatred, at another she can fire them with warlike passion, and at another lift them up to contempt of death itself."[35] (Perhaps this personification of "ensnaring" rhetoric as a female is a prelude to Milton's Eve and her coaxing Adam to sin.) Milton does make the distinction between those who use rhetoric properly and those who do not,[36] which becomes clear when he calls Salmasius the "barbarous rhetorician." We must not condemn rhetoric because Satan used it for evil ends, as anyone else might do. As Milton declares in *Areopagitica,* the things of the world are neutral; what people do with them makes the things good or evil.[37]

Because rhetoric is powerful and can entrap, Milton and the ancients insisted on the orator being a good human being. A good orator means just that, proficient and ethically upright. Milton and the ancients placed a premium on truth. As Milton says, "True eloquence I find to be none but the serious and hearty love of truth."[38] And he says elsewhere, "The highest function of persuasion is to advance truth and cause the audience to accept it."[39] Aristotle goes so far as to say that virtue should manifest itself even if the speech has to suffer: "It is more fitting that a virtuous man should show himself good than that his speech should be painfully exact."[40] Without a good orator to lead the people, it was feared that people would fall into vice. In the *Prolusions,* Milton asserts, "The fact is, Gentlemen, that some few outstanding scholars may have been corrupted by the bad morals of their country and the vulgarity of ignorant men, yet the illiterate masses have often been held to their duty by the efforts of a single learned and wise man."[41]

While Milton wrote a Ramist logic, his ideas about rhetoric are decidedly not Ramist.[42] Supporting this view is the fact that Milton writes about the importance of memory in *Of Education,* whereas Ramist teachings downgraded the significance of memory.[43] And while Walter Ong explains that Ramus grounded his rhetoric in logic, Milton's rhetoric is not constrained by a list of rules, axioms, proofs, or systems derived from logic. Just as classical rhetoric is open, so is Milton's. Milton himself stresses this openness in *Of Education:* "Logic therefore so much as is usefull, is to be referr'd to this due place with all her will coucht heads and Topics, untill it be time to open her contracted palm into a gracefull and ornate Rhetorick taught out the rule of *Plato, Aristotle, Phalereus, Cicero, Hermogenes, Longinus.*"[44] Into his attitude of openness we can fit Milton's dogged support of liberty, and his ability to see both sides of a question, something for which his own oratorical training prepared him.[45] From pamphlets like *Areopagitica,* in which he advises Parliament to keep open the communication of ideas through books, to his own works like *Paradise Lost,* in which Adam and Eve exercise their freedom, Milton continually champions openness. All this talk about openness does not mean that Milton failed to consider situations such as censorship, when openness was not always possible. Milton's world was one in which censorship, along with education, played a prominent role. The epigraph by Patterson that begins this chapter indicates the pervasiveness of censorship, as well as some of the strategies used by writers to keep their texts open while evading the wrath of the censor.

Writing against the censor in Milton's time had serious consequences. Patterson cites one example from 1630 involving Alexander Leighton, author of *Sion's Plea,* a work which sparked further rebelliousness in the 1628 Parliament. "As one of the first symbols of Charles' decision to rule without Parliament . . . , Leighton was fined by the Star Chamber ten thousand pounds for his authorship of *Sion's Plea.*"[46] As described in John Burn's *The Star Chamber: Notices of the Court and Its Proceedings* (1870): "[Leighton] was then transferred to the High Commission Court, to be deprived of his ministry, then to be whipped, pilloried, to lose his ears, his nose slit, his face branded with a double SS for sower of sedition, and lastly sent to the Fleet for life."[47] The SS branding takes on another layer of meaning in the present, and the Leighton case reminds us of the agricultural metaphor for education, for the Star Chamber perceives Leighton as another Cain, a sower of sedition, a tiller who should be feared—in part, because of his cunning with discourse.

I want to suggest that by focusing on poetry, Milton's education program prepares students to deal with polysemous language, and to make use of the dark, inner part of the cornucopia, especially the part where the twist is. Milton writes, "If the language be difficult, so much the better. . . ." So much the better if people avoid the censor and prison, perhaps torture, by knowing about difficult language, the sort of language that can be taken in numerous ways, so that when the censor tries to make a determination, the censor will be confronted with indeterminacy—or at least with what could be taken for double meanings. The Temple of Janus is a place of worship for the poet and for the politician, but it is a place of nightmares for the censor.

$\mathcal{A}$ndgame: Wittgenstein, Bakhtin, and Literary Theory

How many people turn on the radio and leave the room, satisfied with this distant and sufficient noise? Is this absurd? Not in the least. What is essential is not that one particular person speak and another hear, but that, with no one in particular speaking and no one in particular listening, there should nonetheless be speech, and a kind of undefined promise to communicate, guaranteed by the incessant coming and going of solitary words.
—Maurice Blanchot[1]

Samuel Beckett's *Endgame* is, for the most part, a two-character play: Hamm is blind and confined to a wheelchair, and Clov is Hamm's companion and servant. Both find it difficult to muster reasons to go on living. At one point, Clov says, "What is there to keep me here?" "The dialogue," Hamm responds.[2] These lines will serve as a way to bring together the three subjects of this chapter: Ludwig Wittgenstein, Mikhail Bakhtin, and literary theory, although other connections are possible. For example, Wittgenstein and Bakhtin never engaged in a face-to-face dialogue, but Wittgenstein did meet and befriend Bakhtin's brother Nicholas in Cambridge. In fact, Fania Pascal says that Wittgenstein loved Nicholas.[3] Nor did Wittgenstein and Bakhtin read one another's works as far as I can tell, but they both emphasized the importance of the everyday and of dialogue, though not in the sense of dialogue as a binary opposition. This notion of dialogue, emphasized in both of their works, supports a larger claim about the social nature of language: that language functions as the give-and-take between people. This is in opposition to a view of language as a sign system, perhaps even as a grammar. By adhering to the ways language goes on between people, both Bakhtin and Wittgenstein maintain openness, so that there will always be more to say, some way to go on talking.

One of the things that interests me about these two people is the similarity of their thinking in light of their differences: that Wittgenstein's native tongue was German, while Bakhtin's was Russian; that Wittgenstein lived in cosmopolitan locales like Vienna and Cambridge, while Bakhtin worked in revolutionary Russia, creating his most famous work during Stalin's reign, occasionally in exile, often under the scrutiny of the authorities. These "official difficulties" are, in part, why confusion arose about whether Bakhtin had published works under his colleagues' names. You will not find me trying to explain each man's work through his life. So why even consider them together? What is there to keep me here writing about two apparently unrelated people? The dialogue.

I

Wittgenstein began his philosophical career by trying to end it with the only book he published during his lifetime, the *Tractatus Logico-Philosophicus* (1921). The *Tractatus* is Wittgenstein's Endgame. As Richard Rorty says, "Wittgenstein began by thinking that he had made a philosophy so pure that its problems had only to be stated to be solved or dissolved, and so he thought that philosophy had been brought to an end."[4] Wittgenstein himself summed up his attitude at that time in his preface to the *Tractatus:* "What can be said at all can be said clearly, and what we cannot talk about we must pass over in silence. Thus the aim of this book is to draw a limit to thought."[5] Further, he thought he had slain philosophy's Hydra. "I believe myself to have found," he said, "on all essential points, the final solutions of the problems."[6] The *Tractatus* set the boundaries of language by putting everything in order—an order culminating in silence. The final word of the *Tractatus* is "silence" (*schweigen*).

In *Endgame,* Hamm detects that Clov is picking up objects lying on the ground and asks, "What are you doing?" Clov responds, "Putting things in order. I'm going to clear everything away! . . . I love order. It's my dream. A world where all would be silent and still and each thing in its last place, under the last dust."[7] Clov's desire is akin to the desire of those who want to clear up the difficulties in language. They want to take language away to the sterile world of symbolic logic and grammar, away from the loose, cluttered, sometimes Usher-like house of ordinary language, where language's excessiveness cannot be contained, where it keeps spilling out and over, as ungraspable as mercury. Wittgenstein and Bakhtin delve into the wild world of language and criticize those who try to keep themselves and language from spinning out of control. We witness this battle against closure in the later (post-*Tractatus*) Wittgenstein's criticisms of systematic linguistic philosophy and in Bakhtin's arguments against the Russian Formalists, who promoted the idea of a closed structural unity of art works. We are all aware of attempts to construct mathematical languages that eliminate the problems of discourse, multiplicity, and ambiguity; consider the efforts of the medieval Modistae, or of Leibniz, and works such as the Port Royal Grammar (1660), and John Wilkins's *Essay Towards a Real Character and a Philosophical Language* (1668).[8] Some philosophers would like to raze the Tower of Babel, the Home of Heteroglossia, and leave a barren plain in its place. Recall Quine's pun from his *Theories and Things:* "Cognitive discourse at its most drily literal is largely a refinement rather, characteristic of the inner stretches of science. It is an open space in the tropical jungle, created by clearing tropes away."[9] This fear of the looseness of language, the weakness of the *logoi,* can be plotted from Plato to the present.

Of course, Wittgenstein chose not to play out his endgame, and he changed his mind about the *Tractatus* as the end of philosophy, which is why we now talk about the early and later Wittgenstein. In fact, later he says that the mathematical language laid out in the *Tractatus* is but another language-game. Mathematical languages cannot claim any extraordinary status, nor should we regard them as superior to ordinary language. In the collection known as *Remarks on the Foundations of Mathematics,* Wittgenstein questions the singularity and validity of the fundamental and ubiquitous example $2 + 2 = 4$. Using diagrams that illustrate that four x's can be grouped in more than one way, Wittgenstein is able to state plausibly that $2 + 2 + 2 = 4$.[10] Like other language-games, mathematics is characterized by multiplicity and by social agreements. Wittgenstein writes: "The proof makes one structure generate another. It exhibits the generation of one from others. That is all very well—but still it does quite different things in different cases!"[11] Some object that this is regressive relativism, and Wittgenstein responds not with a more rigorous mathematics but with a finger pointing out to what goes on in the world. For example, he says, "I *go through* the proof and then accept its result.—I mean: this is simply what we *do*. This is use and custom among us, or a fact of our natural history. . . . If you draw different conclusions you do indeed get into conflict, e.g., with society, and also with other practical consequences."[12] As David Bloor suggests, Wittgenstein's is a social theory of knowledge: "If what he [Wittgenstein] says is true, or anywhere near the truth, the great categories of objectivity and rationality can never look the same again. Think how often our polemical appeals to these two things depend on our portraying them as forms of external compulsion. A social theory of knowledge changes all this. Objectivity and rationality must be things that we forge for ourselves as we construct a form of collective life."[13]

Whereas some see Wittgenstein opening the world to view, others see him providing yet another methodology. Henry Staten's Wittgenstein represents a particular method called "destabilization": "Wittgenstein is primarily not making arguments or teaching new concepts, though much of what he writes certainly looks like those things; rather he is instructing us all in a skill, a method, a strategy."[14] If we accept Staten's claim that Wittgenstein shows us a method, then Wittgenstein exhibits a free and open method, one that would be difficult to call *one*, and also one that would be difficult to call systematic. Staten leans on the word "method," because he wants to talk about Wittgenstein's *grammar*. In Wittgenstein's examples, people build, play, go to the store to purchase items. In that way, we read about people "knowing how to go on," not people "destabilizing" texts or societies.

Wittgenstein's is not a philosophy of Anything Goes—just as you cannot move the pieces on a chessboard any which way, even though you could move numerous pieces when it is your turn. You are supposed to follow the rules, which you learn from more experienced players and through practice. Not that you would move a bishop the way the queen should be moved (that too could become a game, were you able to get your partner to understand), but you will learn what moves are appropriate to what stage of the game. Chess contains its own temporality, which is why chess players talk about openings, midgames, and endgames. Still, the number of possible moves you could make within the rules is legion, even in the endgame when fewer pieces are on the board.

Endgames highlight the richness of possibilities, as suggested in the truncated dialogue in Beckett's play. Toward the end of the play, when Clov is holding an alarm clock, Hamm asks, "What are you doing?" And Clov answers, "Winding up," which could mean he is beginning, or beginning to end. Starting or finishing? How do we decide? Certainly the grammar isn't going to help, anymore than it would if you were confronted with Frege's dilemma over the morning star and the evening star. What to do? Wittgenstein's advice is to look and see what is the case. In the *Blue Book,* Wittgenstein says, "We are unable clearly to circumscribe the concepts we use; not because we don't know their real definition, but because there is no real 'definition' to them."[15] There's no real definition as to what Clov means by "winding up," but attending to the context of Clov's statement will help, and we might find out that Clov means both; that is, that he is both starting and finishing. Hamm comes to understand Clov through further dialogue. Similarly, in chess, a player's move is understood or misunderstood depending on whether the other player's response to the move is appropriate. In chess, as in language, one must face the consequences of a wrong move.

II

Bakhtin focuses on the dialogical nature of understanding, on the notion of game, and on the importance of social and historical contexts of language. He writes, "There are no 'neutral' words and forms—words and forms that can belong to 'no one'; language has been completely taken over, shot through with intentions and accents. For any individual consciousness living in it, language is not an abstract system of normative forms but rather a concrete heteroglot conception of the world. All words have the 'taste' of a profession, a genre, a tendency, a party, a particular work, a particular person, a generation, an age group, the day and hour. Each word tastes of the context and contexts in which it has lived its socially charged life."[16] If one wants to figure something out, one looks to the world, to what is manifest, out in plain view. This seems to apply to Wittgenstein as well, who uses conversation as the model of understanding. Throughout Wittgenstein's works, such as the *Philosophical Investigations,* he uses the dialogue form—not extended dialogues with actual historical figures as in the case of Plato, but imaginary figures in miniature dialogues. To test out his ideas, Wittgenstein invents interlocutors who present counterarguments and questions, setting up situations in which an implicit "suppose that someone were to say . . ." is at work. Such an approach reminds one of a few old meanings (according to the second edition of *The Oxford English Dictionary*) of "and." At some time, "and" meant "if; suppose that." We might call this use of hypothetical situations Wittgenstein's style, a style that includes others. Granted, sometimes the counterarguments are quite feeble, and Wittgenstein takes pleasure in poking fun, as he does in *On Certainty:* "What is the belief that all human beings have parents based on? On experience. And how can I base this sure belief on experience? Well, I base it not only on the fact that I have known the parents of certain people but on everything that I have learned about the sexual life of human beings and their anatomy and physiology: also on what I have heard and seen of animals. But then is that really a proof?"[17] The appeal here is to what one has heard or seen, to one's own experience, and to raise experience to a criterion for making sense of things. This criterion leads both Wittgenstein and Bakhtin to disagree with Freud, who is seen as overly concerned with the internal. In considering Bakhtin's objections to Freud, one must keep in mind that, in part, Bakhtin is reacting to Soviet psychologists' appropriation of Freud and their attempts to make Freud into a dialectical materialist. Still, Bakhtin objects to Freud's turn to the internal, the psyche, or the mind, at the expense of the relationship between the I and the Other. As Clark and Holquist explain in their biography of Bakhtin, Freud failed "to recognize the degree to which language is socialized and belongs not to the individual but to the group. Freud sought to monologize the nature of language, which was a necessary step if language was to be internalized in the consciousness as Freud described it. He saw the language of the unconscious as being at war with the language of consciousness, but the battle was fought out within the individual psyche."[18]

Freud conceives of the unconscious as preceding, or external to, language. Yet, our only access to the unconscious is through language. In place of Freud's conscious/unconscious distinction, Bakhtin substitutes what he calls an official and unofficial consciousness. What is official or unofficial is a social function, not an individual, private one, because as Todorov puts it, "For Bakhtin, at the bottom of man [sic] we find not the Id but the other."[19] To quote Bakhtin: "We appraise ourselves from the point of view of others. . . . I cannot perceive myself in my external aspect."[20] Todorov goes on to explain, "Only someone else's gaze can give me the appearance of being consubstantial with the external world. For only the other can be totally surrounded, and explored lovingly in all of his or her limits."[21] And again Bakhtin: "I am conscious of myself and become myself only while revealing myself for another, through another, and with the help of another. . . . Looking inside himself, he looks *into the eyes of another* or *with the eyes of another*."[22] (The face-to-face scene also takes us back to some more old meanings of "and": viz., "facing, fronting.") Thus character is social and public, not personal and private. This is an appropriate place to return to Bruns, who makes a similar point: "It appears to be the case that society reserves for itself the last right or authority for the fixing of character, in the sense that what you are, or what you appear to be, slips naturally into the domain of invention: what is said about you."[23]

Bruns seems to corroborate Wittgenstein's private language argument, which goes something like this: Just as you cannot make up your own rules while playing chess, so a language that only one person could understand would be meaningless, senseless. In what are called his *Remarks on the Philosophy of Psychology*, Wittgenstein builds his case against worries about intentions and what goes on in private, in the "mind." He writes, "'I'd like to know what he's thinking of.' But now ask yourself this—apparently irrelevant—question. 'Why does what is going on in him, in his mind, interest me at all, supposing that something is going on?' (The devil take what's going on inside him!)"[24] As for individual motives, Wittgenstein says, "We judge the motive of an act by what its author tells us, by the report of eye witnesses, by the preceding history" (I, no. 631). An interesting remark that furthers this argument is Wittgenstein's assertion that "the dagger which Macbeth sees before him is not an imagined dagger" (II, no. 85). Clearly, Macbeth behaves as if the dagger were real, and that behavior is the evidence we use to talk about Macbeth (and whatever internal states some might attribute to him). We come to understand Macbeth because he does things we can see, says things we can hear, and because he is one of us. We know him because we have some familiarity with human beings. "To be sure," Wittgenstein says, "one could imagine seeing human life in a film, or being allowed merely to observe life without participating in it. Anyone who did this would then understand human life as we understand the life of fish or even of plants. We can't talk about the joy and sorrow . . . of fish" (II, no. 29).

Perhaps the power of the two men's views emerges in the following quotations. First Bakhtin in "Art and Answerability": "I have to answer with my own life for what I have experienced and understood in art, so that everything I have experienced and understood would not remain ineffectual in my life. But answerability entails guilt, or liability to blame."[25] This sounds close to what Levinas has to say about the human condition, about how we are hostages the moment we enter the world. Now Wittgenstein: "The way to solve the problem you see in life is to live in a way that will make what is problematic disappear." In the Wittgenstein quotation, you can still hear the *Tractatus* and his desire to make problems disappear. But he couldn't have his wish. Questions haunted him, like Hamm's questions to Clov in *Endgame,* not rhetorical questions. A rhetorical question is like the heart in the following exchange between Hamm and Clov:

> *Hamm:* Last night I saw inside my breast. There was a big sore.
> *Clov:* Pah! You saw your heart.
> *Hamm:* No, it was living.

I bring in the rhetorical question here because I think Wittgenstein and Bakhtin attend to rhetorical considerations such as audience, context, and desire for agreement—not that these things constitute a definition of rhetoric, but something more along the lines of a description, what you might say if someone asked you what rhetoric looks like.

To be a rhetorician means not only knowing ways to bring about silence, but also knowing how to go on, how to keep the conversation going. This suggests that rhetoric can be an andgame, the wish to keep things going. "Ands" allow you to continue the dialogue, which for Hamm is life. When Clov leaves and the dialogue ends, so does Hamm. There is nothing to keep him here. As long as the dialogue continues, Hamm has hope of meaning:

> *Hamm:* What is happening?
> *Clov:* Something is taking its course.
> *Hamm:* Clov!
> *Clov:* What is it?
> *Hamm:* We're not beginning to . . . to . . . mean something?
> *Clov:* Mean something! You and I mean something! Ah, that's a good one.

III

The endgame to this piece might not result in meaning and will not produce finality, given the persistence of the quotidian. What brings us to sorrow from the perspective of Wittgenstein and Bakhtin is the renunciation of the everyday, the continual efforts to go beyond the mundane. More, both these thinkers locate our very salvation in the everyday, not that we will probably more often choose the extraordinary should it be offered. Morson and Emerson afford a thorough account of Bakhtin's views on everydayness: "For Bakhtin . . . the everyday is a sphere of constant activity, the source of all social change and individual creativity. The prosaic is the truly interesting and the ordinary is what is truly noteworthy."[26] By this point, those in the academy know about Bakhtin's attention to the street, e.g., his writings on carnivals and clowns.

Stanley Cavell approaches Wittgenstein this way: "[Wittgenstein] depicts our everyday encounters with philosophy, say with our ideals, as brushes with skepticism, wherein the ancient task of philosophy, to awaken us, or say bring us to our senses, takes the form of returning us to the everyday, the ordinary. . . ."[27] Cavell also says that Wittgenstein appreciates—a strange verb in this context— the threat of skepticism about the everyday, skepticism that is not to be eradicated. Many, including myself, have turned to the *Philosophical Investigations* for an antidote to skepticism, but this seems misguided, as misguided as the antidote becomes at the end of Hawthorne's "Rappaccini's Daughter." Cavell's efforts draw our attention to skepticism, but he does not portray skepticism as a dragon that we can expect to slay with the properly potent philosophical weapons.

Wittgenstein says in the *Investigations:* "Philosophical problems are solved, not by giving new information, but by arranging what we have always known" (no. 109). One of the usual slaps at Wittgenstein consists in laughing (and I do not want to squelch this laughter, but encourage it) at his examples and their everydayness, as if anyone could have thought of them, and I take it that this is one of the points. If you take philosophy to be some form of esoteric discourse, a passage about someone calling for a slab is bound to sound silly. But ordinary language philosophy invites ordinary human beings to it, not that ordinary language philosophy is simple-minded, or that it lacks a specialized vocabulary, but that it has the potential to be, say, democratic. Here is what Cavell says that Wittgenstein teaches us: "Skepticism, or rather the threat of it, is no more *incurable* than the capacities to think and to talk, though these capacities too, chronically, cause us sorrow" (UA, 54). Further,

Cavell warns us that Wittgenstein wants to return us to the every-day, but we should not expect the everyday to seem familiar; it will be more like seeing the everyday as if for the first time, because "Wittgenstein's appeal . . . to the everyday finds the (actual) every-day to be as pervasive a scene of illusion and trance and artificiality (of need) as Plato or Rousseau or Marx or Thoreau had found" (UA, 46). Again and again, Cavell points to the task of the philoso-pher to awaken us, as if we are sometimes dead to the world.

According to Cavell, Wittgenstein in the *Investigations* offers the chance to return to the everyday and to go on, which means philosophy has the chance to go on as well. To Cavell's credit, he realizes that another one of the ways of going on, of dealing with skepticism, looks like massive denial at times, as in Wittgenstein's *Remarks on the Foundations of Mathematics* when he says, "Is no demon deceiving us at present? Well, if he is, it doesn't matter. What the eye doesn't see the heart doesn't grieve over."[28] Hans Blumen-berg, who knows how philosophy occasionally benefits from being an art of resignation and renunciation, makes this case powerful not only by using such passages as the one above, but also by appealing to information from Wittgenstein's private life, such as a statement made on Wittgenstein's last day in 1951, when after a life of unrest, depression, and thoughts of suicide, Wittgenstein said: "Tell them that I had a wonderful life."[29]

I am not going to resist the temptation here to turn to the classic film *It's a Wonderful Life* (1946), which demonstrates the movement between skepticism and the recovery from skepticism, between despair and the hope that comes from thinking about another form of life, say a life in which one had never played a part. George Bailey's return to his life after confronting nonexistence seems to be the sort of return to the everyday Wittgenstein tries to bring us to, the kind that is like being reborn to the world. Of course, we all know that nothing has changed from the time George decides he is worth more dead than alive to the time he returns home with his new perspective on life; he even retains a touch of his skepticism, exclaiming, "Mary! Let me touch you—you're real—you're real!"[30] Nevertheless, something significant has changed. Maybe this something should be called seeing things differently, or just seeing (that one is not alone). Actually, much goes on in the world while George wonders whether to return to it. For instance, his community does not turn its back on George and his family, but takes up rescue efforts. *It's a Wonderful Life* is not the story of George Bailey's solitary consciousness.

By comparing Wittgenstein's deathbed statement to the story of George Bailey, I hope to vindicate Wittgenstein somewhat, to take him partially out of the context Blumenberg has constructed, and to push him toward the context of E. M. Cioran's claim that "we cannot reconquer life nor revel in it without having first abolished it." Facing death, Wittgenstein could have gone through a George Bailey-like transformation, and if we can accept George Bailey's reanimation to his life, why should we deny truth to Wittgenstein's claim that he had a wonderful life? Why should we balk at the thought that we can be Lazarus before we are dead? Keep in mind the distinction between an endgame and finality.

$\mathscr{A}$ Reading of Derrida's "White Mythology"

I don't want realism. I want magic! [*Mitch laughs*] Yes, yes, magic! I try to give that to people. I misrepresent things to them. I don't tell the truth, I tell what ought to be the truth. And if that is sinful, then let me be damned for it! *Don't turn the light on!*—Blanche DuBois, *A Streetcar Named Desire*

Granted, these are images, metaphors, parables, means of speech that are props used in following a direction of thought, nothing that shall or can be kept forever, they are something that just come about as words come if you want to say something.—Hans-Georg Gadamer[1]

In every claim to bring myth to an end the more far-reaching, if only implied, claim is exposed that one brings *myth* [as such] to an end when one displays *one* final myth. The evidence that it is the last myth requires a totality, a perfection whose fateful effectiveness consists precisely, not in the fulfillment of the intention that commands us to forgo further production of myths, but rather in its making it possible for the first time to experience the fascination that does not allow one to rest until one has imitated the model, equalled the standard that it sets, or even surpassed it.—Hans Blumenberg[2]

How does one approach Derrida? As Allan Megill puts it, "No one of us can hope to fulfill the conditions for reading him properly."[3] Derrida does not play "by the rules," which means he does not play *our* language-game, nor the language-game of the West—the game of metaphysics—which Derrida sees as exhausted anyway. "Metaphysicians prefer to use the most worn out words from natural language" (211; 3), he writes.[4] Still, Derrida chooses to write about what he calls the metaphysicians of the West, who use metaphors that contain the death of philosophy. Given that Derrida has recalled these metaphors for our inspection and suspicion, he implicates himself in this death. And if one were to support Derrida, one might say, as so many other deconstructionists have, that he deconstructs himself. In other words, he plays by his own rules, often allowing language to rule in order to demonstrate how well the ruling works, especially well on his own work. At times, Derrida seems to be playing two games at once, a kind of "double session," something like writing with both hands simultaneously.

What is the occasion for writing about Derrida? For one, he is—at least in literature departments in North America—the most well-known living Continental philosopher, and perhaps the most influential. "White Mythology" takes up matters that concern all of philosophy, or perhaps one should say all of metaphysics.

What question does "White Mythology" answer? Is it fair to say the question could be: What is at the bottom of metaphysics? Or: What is the ground upon which Western metaphysics has been built? Or: What is the essence of language used to talk about Western metaphysics? (Like Gadamer, I am not sure what Derrida means by metaphysics.)[5] Or: Why should we think the use of metaphor yields truth?

Derrida's essay seems to focus on what has *not moved* in Western metaphysics, that the metaphor of light constitutes a fixed theme, or ubiquitous motif, that one can latch onto regardless of the occasions on which the metaphysical writings Derrida analyzes emerge. In effect, Derrida says "Hold the bus!" The bus here is metaphor, which means movement. In "The *Retrait* of Metaphor"—in part an essay that responds to Paul Ricoeur's reading of "White Mythology" in Ricoeur's *The Rule of Metaphor*—Derrida sets the essay in motion by commenting on the meaning of *metaphorikos,* "still designating today, in what one calls 'modern' Greek, that which concerns the means of transportation."[6] In the version of the essay that appears in *Enclitic,* there is a representation of a collection of cars, trucks, and buses above the first full paragraph of the text. By the end of this chapter, I will have acquired a transfer from Derrida's buses to *A Streetcar Named Desire,* but first we must ride the bus a while.

Actually, there is no getting off this bus. Derrida characterizes the situation this way: "I can only stop the engines of this floating vehicle which is here my discourse, which would still be the best means of abandoning it to its unforeseeable drifting. The drama, for this is a drama, is that even if I had decided no longer to speak metaphorically about metaphor, I would not achieve it, it would continue to go on without me in order to make me speak, to ventriloquize me, metaphorize me. Other ways of saying, other ways of responding to, rather, my first questions. What is happening *with* metaphor? Well, everything: there is nothing that does not happen with metaphor and by metaphor" (pp. 7–8). Here, Derrida describes the Heideggerian language-bus. On that bus, one doesn't get on or off. Rather, you stand in the street and suddenly the *bus* picks you up and takes you places you cannot imagine, places where you can feel lost. Derrida knows about the ride language can take you on, but he wants temporarily to put on the brakes: "I am going to make the greatest possible effort to slow the skidding" (p. 8). In his essays that explicitly address metaphor, Derrida prefers not to look and see what is the case with metaphor, i.e., what metaphor *does* to people, how it affects them, persuades them, moves them to tears, delights them, takes possession of them—the way the metaphor of light seems to have done to many metaphysicians. Derrida discusses metaphor as a trope, a rhetorical figure in a language system. Perhaps this comes about because Derrida is dealing with metaphor *in writing,* metaphor *in the text* of philosophy. Elsewhere, Derrida displays his awareness of what metaphor can do to others, of words' wounding power, such as in his criticisms of John Searle in "Limited Inc."

In the essay I am trying to understand, Derrida tells us the *final* myth of Western philosophy, which is that Western philosophy condemns itself by being "metaphysics—the white mythology which reassembles and reflects the culture of the West: the white man takes his own mythology, Indo-European mythology, his own *logos,* that is, the *mythos* of his idiom, for the universal form of that he must still wish to call Reason" (213; 4). Derrida is a white man who writes philosophy, who also wants to say that he is something other than a white man who writes philosophy. He is the one willing to "risk meaning nothing."[7]

One of the things I want to take up in this chapter is Derrida's final myth—white mythology. Along with Gadamer, "I would like to know what understanding [*Verstehen*]—and also, which is implicit in it, reading with understanding—has to do with metaphysics" (p. 96). In other words, I would like to know what philosophical hermeneutics has to do with white mythology. Also, I want to consider Derrida's view of myth in relation to what Hans Blumenberg has to say on the topic in *Work on Myth*. In Gadamer's essay "Plato's Unwritten Dialectic," Gadamer says that "differences are possible relationships." What will be at work in this chapter is a continual bringing of Derrida into relationships.

Derrida recalls the Enlightenment prejudice against myth, in which one juxtaposes myth and reason in order to denigrate myth if only by citing the obvious: that myth is primitive and has not undergone refinement through progress. Derrida seeks to establish that for all its "rhetorical" power and insistence on Reason, Western philosophy is stalled at the unenlightened level of myth. Polyphilos, speaking for Derrida (who ventriloquizes himself), says, "By an odd fate, the very metaphysicians who think to escape the world of appearances are constrained to live perpetually in allegory" (213; 4). Later, Derrida asserts that the "issue is to deconstruct practically the *philosophical* opposition between philosophy and myth, between *logos* and *mythos*."[8]

Almost fifteen years before Derrida's "White Mythology," Hans Blumenberg—who, in *Work on Myth*, also denies a split between *logos* and *mythos*—published "*Licht als Metapher der Wahrheit*" (1957), which presents a historical overview of the metaphor of light in metaphysics, though Blumenberg's slant on the matter differs from Derrida's. The point here is not that Blumenberg comes before Derrida in this matter and therefore deserves precedence, but that

Blumenberg offers an angle that Derrida does not. Derrida stresses the overuse and exhaustion of the metaphor of light, which borrows on a bankrupt, worn-out image. For Derrida, metaphor, as used by philosophers, appeals to some "primitive" meaning, some first sensual experience. And this invoking of a "primitive" meaning leads to a "progressive erosion" of that meaning, so that metaphysics becomes the building of metaphors of metaphors. Metaphysics turns in on itself, cannibalizes itself in language.

Derrida claims that "natural light, and all the axioms it brings into our field of vision is never subjected to the most radical doubt" (267; 48). He thus begins by adopting a stance of suspicion. Conversely, Blumenberg begins by concentrating on the positive results that come from using this metaphor. He writes, "For declarative capability and subtle transformational possibilities the light metaphor is incomparable. From its beginnings, the history of metaphysics has made use of its attributes in order to give the last, concrete, no longer tangible facts an appropriate reference."9 In contrast to Derrida, Blumenberg positions this metaphor centrally in the language of metaphysics due to its expressive possibilities, or its potential for bringing a plenitude of language to expression. In other words, metaphor gives us something to say. According to Blumenberg, "What we call 'history' in a fundamental sense, stands always in opposition to the elementary inertia of the means of testimony in which the basic change of interpretation of reality not only manifests itself, but also primarily can bring itself to articulation for itself [*sich selbst für sich selbst zur Artikulation bringen*]."10 Where Derrida speaks of exhaustion, Blumenberg finds abundance. For Derrida, the flowers of rhetoric wilt in the sun under the constant exposure of heliotropes, but Blumenberg's flowers bud perennially, if only through his name. Blumenberg bears down on the basic usefulness of these metaphors for coming to understand things through language, for helping matters, especially abstract ones, to hang together. The light metaphor familiarizes reality (read this "reality" as Blumenberg's absolutism of reality) for us. Naturally, Derrida knows this, as he demonstrates by asking in the very beginning of his essay, "How can we make this sensible except by metaphor?" (209; 1). Metaphor itself is a metaphor, so that whatever backs up philosophy cannot be tracked down, and this, according to Rodolphe Gasché, "signifies a *mise en abyme* of the philosophical concept of metaphor."[11] What wants to be asked here is whether Derrida sides with Nietzsche, who insists that all language is metaphor. If that is the case, then we must read Derrida differently.

According to Derrida, metaphysics is white mythology, and is always caught up in seeking the truth, though mythology forgoes truth according to Blumenberg.[12] "The 'naked truth' is not what life can live with" (110), Blumenberg posits. The entire movement of myth covers the unbearable truth in order to make life bearable by allowing the unspeakable (e.g., why there is something rather than nothing—Blumenberg's example that echoes Heidegger) to enter discourse. Metaphor furnishes human beings with a means of transforming the unspeakable into a narratable story. Nonetheless, this is not the time to equate stories with fiction, but to substitute 'significance' for truth, and to recognize that myths inhabit a different space from most stories. Blumenberg tells us, "The significance of myth is not recognizable as something fictional, because it has no nameable author, because it comes from afar and does not lay claim to a particular chronological position" (75). On this account, Derrida errs in attributing the myth of light to particular authors—to the authors he labels white Indo-European metaphysicians—for myth has no author.

Myth prevents everything from being called into question. As Blumenberg says, "[Myths] make things unquestionable. . . . Myths are answers to questions without permitting further questions" (126; 248). This putting things out of question that myth accomplishes allows for sufficient stability in the world, helps human beings feel at home in the world. A fact Blumenberg dwells on in *Work on Myth*, and one that we should wonder about here, is why the planets in *our* solar system have received names from mythology, but distant stars and objects are still referred to by numbers and letters. And even in this century, with the discovery of another planet, the astronomers still give the planet a mythological name—Pluto.

In our time, theory functions in the same way myth did before we thought we were beyond myth. Blumenberg says: "Theory is the better adapted mode of mastering the episodic *tremenda* of recurring world events. But leisure and dispassion in viewing the world, which theory presupposes, are already results of that millenniums-long work of myth itself, which told of the monstrous as something that is far in the past and has been forced back to the edge of the world" (26). Myth forces everything to the edge because myth occupies everything; it seems ubiquitous through its "indefiniteness of dating and localization" (96). Blumenberg would agree that in myth human beings seek stability, but not by way of an ultimate ground, but something more radical—viz., the pluperfect. Blumenberg speaks not of origins but of the past's past, the pluperfect.

Deconstructionists know that they cannot shake the *archai* of myth, inasmuch as myths have no *archai,* no origins. Derrida is not after origins, for he wants to show metaphysicians looking for origins when such origins cannot be grasped, especially certain origins of metaphors. To the image of erosion, Derrida adds a numismatic metaphor: the wearing down of a coin. What gets worn down is the "original" image of sense that is appealed to by using metaphor; metaphor borrows from this "original." As in an exchange of money, the money permits one to purchase something of greater value, and one rubs up against money only to get at something else. By using a metaphor, we exchange words to get at something else, something more.

Derrida presents his case here, as he does so often in this essay—through the mouth of another, in this instance, Saussure. "To determine what five-franc piece is worth one must therefore know: (1) that it can be exchanged for a fixed quantity of a different thing, e.g., bread, and (2) that it can be compared with a similar value of the same system, e.g., a one-franc piece, or with coins of another system (a dollar, etc.). In *the same way* a word can be exchanged for something dissimilar, an idea . . ." (218; 8).

To give this example a Gödelian twist, I introduce the work of J.S.G. Boggs, an artist who draws paper money and tries to exchange the bills to pay for, say, his meal at a restaurant. For example, Boggs draws a hundred-dollar bill (the face only) and then tells the waiter: "I am an artist, and I drew this. It took me many hours to do it, and it's certainly worth something I'm assigning it an arbitrary price, which just happens to coincide with its face value—one hundred dollars. That means that if you decide to accept it as full payment for our meal, you're going to have to give me thirteen dollars in change. So you have to make up your mind whether you think this piece of art is worth more or less than this regular one-hundred dollar bill. It's entirely up to you."[13] One of the things to notice here is that we have a social interaction, not the operation of a system. Boggs wants to throw a wrench into the "system" of money and value by insisting that people make choices about value and about representation. What one *does* confers value, rather than objects' containing intrinsic value. Furthermore, Boggs's work, once extrapolated, pushes matters into a Derridean-like crisis by forcing us to ponder a situation in which coins and bills are "cashed in." In other words, what happens on the day when people want the value the money represents? Since we are no longer on a gold or a silver standard, what is it that backs up money? In his article on Boggs, Robert Krulwich, an economics correspondent, explains the pre-cariousness inherent in these sorts of exchanges. Krulwich says:

> One of the interesting things is that paper money circulates but it doesn't drive out the gold, just as the gold didn't completely drive out barter. Everything exists side by side. Eventually, you begin to get checking, which is a method whereby I sign a piece of paper instructing my bank to give you some of its kind of paper. . . . Little by little, the various backings of the coins are withdrawn—you can no longer redeem your check for a paper bill that can be redeemed for gold or silver. Now all you can exchange your bill for is a new bill. . . . Nowadays, a half a trillion dollars changes hands every day—although no hands are involved, and, in a sense, no dollars either, and not even numbers really. It's just binary sequences of pulses racing between computers. . . .
>
> In the midst of all that, this fellow Boggs has found a way to illustrate—to act out—the essential nature of exchanges and money. He forces us to see, among other things, how it's all a fiction, there's nothing backing it, it's all an act of faith.[14]

This is Derrida's point about metaphysics: *In the same way* as money, the metaphors of metaphysics have no backing; and if one day someone tried to "cash in" the metaphors of metaphysics, the person would find nothing, except maybe faith. Yet, given this context, the suggestion seems to be that acts of faith are nothing, and that trust is worthless. Trust and faith come under skeptical attack because we cannot attach objects to them, as if objects were all that could be valued. In "White Mythology," we do not find people making exchanges, establishing bonds, finding value—human values rather than values that are limited to the materials exchanged—for the text restricts itself to what goes on in philosophy and to how much philosophical writing depends on the reader's trust. As Hartman explains in *Saving the Text:* "One should not talk of understanding . . . as if it were a matter of rules or techniques that become intuitive and quasi-silent. There is, of course, an internalization; but the life-situation of the interpreter has to deal with riddles as well as puzzles: what is sought is often the readiness to take and give words in trust, rather than the answer to a problem."[15] Part of this trust includes an acknowledgment that a large part of everyday conversation consists of exchanges of plagiary. Those familiar with Hermes know about "borrowing."

One could say that people, and what they do, comprise the backing, the supports of both money and metaphysics. Do not mistake this for an entirely anthropocentric reading, for once we return to the pluperfect, I can appeal to Blumenberg's insight that myth is not anthropocentric (in the sense that myth is not *centered* on humans). Instead, myth emerges from human beings' awareness that there are forces beyond their understanding and control. One becomes implicated in something that is more than oneself. Anthropologist Horst Kurnitzky has surmised that the myth relating to money originated in substitutions for sacrifices in ancient rituals. Kurnitzky proposes that there came a time when human beings put an end to human sacrifices by substituting animal sacrifices, and that this sort of substitution served as a model for later exchanges and trades.[16] Boggs exacerbates the notion of substitution and compels those involved in the exchange to reconsider the literal meaning of money.

From the literal, metaphor. Both Derrida and Nietzsche bypass the distinction between the literal and the metaphorical—between what is overlooked (the literal) and what is raised up (*relevé*) and brought to our attention (metaphor). Boggs makes people attend to the literal level, to *look* at the bills he has drawn in relation to the bills that continually pass in and out of hands without thought. Perhaps we could call the literal the taken-for-granted. In his study of metaphor, Ricoeur draws the line here: "The criterion of delimitation is clear: the metaphorical sense of a word presupposes contrast with a literal sense. . . . The study of the lexicalization of metaphor . . . greatly contributes to dispelling the false enigma of worn-out metaphor."[17] For Ricoeur, metaphors reanimate dead language and offer new meaning. Still, at least in this instance, Ricoeur remains locked into an epistemological model for metaphor. What is literal and what is taken as metaphor depends on the situation, on the way speakers and listeners read one another.

To inject a further distinction, I turn again to Blumenberg. It seems safe to say that the light metaphor is paradigmatic. Distinguishing types of metaphor, Blumenberg would call the light metaphor an absolute metaphor, because, he says, absolute metaphors have *histories*. "They have histories in a radical sense as concepts, because the historical change of metaphor brings to light the metakinetic historical horizons of sense [*Sinnhorizonte*] and the ways of viewing themselves, within which concepts experience their modifications."[18] The staying power of the light metaphor indicates that something else besides exhaustion, or a wearing away, is going on. Why, with the advent of modern science, has myth, white mythology in particular, not come to an end?

Over a hundred years have passed since Nietzsche's "On Truth and Lies in a Nonmoral Sense" (1873), in which he too told us that all language is figurative, a conglomeration of arbitrary designations. It seems germane to attend to this text since it takes on great importance in "White Mythology." What does it mean that Nietzsche's essay, so significant to backing up Derrida's essay, exhibits extensive usury? Geoff Waite showed me that Nietzsche built his essay from other texts, like Gustav Gerber's *Die Sprache als Kunst*. For example, we find the following passage in Nietzsche's essay:

"How could we still dare to say 'the stone is hard,' as if 'hard' were something otherwise familiar to us, and not merely a totally subjective stimulation!"[19] This is the very same example used in Gerber's text, though Nietzsche offers no attribution, no mention of the human exchange that took place.[20] Many of Gerber's examples can be found in Nietzsche's text, which Nietzsche dedicated to a friend. Philippe Lacoue-Labarthe and others reconstruct this intertextuality in the same issue of *Poetique* in which Derrida's "*La mythologie blanche*" appears.

For critics like J. Hillis Miller, Nietzsche's essay teaches us how to be deconstructive readers. "Insofar as the reader takes the metaphor literally and assumes the truth is an effaced coin, he [sic] is doing what the image tells him not to do. He is forgetting the aberrant ground of the figure, the way it is a stammering translation of something which remains unknown and unknowable."[21] One of the most famous of these figures for deconstruction is Nietzsche's umbrella. In *Éperons,* Derrida plays out a sentence from Nietzsche's unpublished manuscript: "*J'ai oublié mon parapluie.*" He says, "One day though we shall perhaps know the significant context of this umbrella," and indeed, Geoffrey Waite has provided such a context.[22] That the umbrella has *a* history is not what Derrida says he is after. Derrida's point is that the meaning of the sentence will always remain "inaccessible." We will not be able to get back to the sentence's origins, any more than one could recapture the origins of myth. The opening of the umbrella blocks out the light one wants to shed on the questions about the umbrella. One final example will show what happens when people refuse to put limits on their knowledge. If you allow me the freedom of play that you grant Derrida, it is time to turn from "*La mythologie blanche*" to "*La mythologie Blanche DuBois.*"

A Streetcar Named Desire, not regularly thought of as a text of metaphysics, employs the light metaphor and takes us into a world occupied by human beings who are neither philosophers nor literary critics. In the play's first scene, Tennessee Williams tells us about Blanche DuBois. "There is something about her uncertain manner, as well as her white clothes, that suggests a moth."[23] As we know, moths hover around light, and Blanche's world depends upon a subtle interplay of light and darkness. "Her delicate beauty must avoid a strong light," Williams says in the stage directions.

Williams fills the play with light metaphors, and Blanche's concern about the right kind of lighting. For instance, when she is with Mitch (Harold Mitchell) after a date, Blanche says, "I want to create—*joie de vivre!* I'm lighting a candle."[24] Naturally, everyone accepts Blanche's attention to lighting, until skepticism about her sets in toward the end of the play. Then Mitch says to her, "You never want to go out till after six and then it's always some place that's not lighted much."[25] Even Blanche's response to this connects up with light: "There is some obscure meaning in this but I fail to catch it."

By the end of the play we learn that Blanche has survived by fashioning a mythology about herself, one that hangs on the regulation of the light metaphor and hinges on the faith and trust of others, the sort of acceptance Blanche receives from her sister Stella. As Blumenberg says about myths—i.e., that they put themselves out of question—so Blanche wants to keep her mythology out of question: "Don't turn the light on!" Likewise, at the end of the play, Stella puts out of question what went on between Stanley and Blanche, so that she can continue her marriage with Stanley.

What worries me is the intolerance toward "*La mythologie Blanche DuBois,*" the merciless drive to expose her origins, to find out what she is really about, to turn the light on to show that she is something worn out, like the metaphors of metaphysics. There is plenty of light already with which to see Blanche without ripping the shade off the lamp. "But," as Levinas tells us, "we want only a knowledge completely tested through our own evidence. We do not want to undertake anything without knowing everything, and nothing can become known to us unless we have gone and seen for ourselves, regardless of the misadventures of the exploration. We want to live dangerously, but in security, in the world of truths. Seen in this manner, the temptation of temptation is . . . philosophy itself."[26] Perhaps that is the lesson of "*La mythologie blanche.*"

$\mathcal{A}$gainst Clarity: Hermeneutics and Writing

All narratives are capable of darkness.—Frank Kermode[1]

Everything that lives, not vegetative life alone, emerges from darkness and, however strong its natural tendency to thrust itself into the light, it nevertheless needs the security of darkness to grow at all.—Hannah Arendt[2]

The *Phaedrus* reminds us that all writing is merely a "reminder": the real activity of teaching and learning goes on not on the page but in the souls of people.—Martha Nussbaum[3]

I

This chapter concerns what will be called a dark theory of writing, set against clear writing so often taught in today's writing courses. It is an invitation to a labyrinth, which, according to Greek mythology, is a place that can teach you how to make your way in the dark, in a place of danger. Yet, one must always keep in mind the labyrinth's positive hermeneutical function: it is a place to lose oneself, or put more familiarly, a place where one can get lost. To understand my direction in this chapter is to stand in the shoes of Daedalus, which is not to say that to be in his shoes means that you cannot get lost in the labyrinth. Yes, Daedalus constructed the labyrinth, but King Minos imprisoned him therein, for Minos had the insight that Joseph Leo Koerner mentions—i.e., that Daedalus could not both *know* and *experience* the labyrinth. To look at the blueprints of a labyrinth is not the same as being *inside* a labyrinth.

This is an excellent example of one of the differences between outsiders and insiders: outsiders can have knowledge about the inside, but only insiders have the experience.

I want to connect the image and the stories of labyrinths to education, particularly to teaching students to write. In the first part of this chapter I will depend for guidance on Koerner's *Die Suche nach dem Labyrinth*.[4] Koerner tells us that the labyrinth is as old as humankind, that historical evidence about its existence does not begin with the story of Daedalus, but with the Egyptians from whom Daedalus learned about constructing labyrinths. According to Koerner, "To wander into the labyrinth means to experience chaos and the alienating dimension of time."[5] It is a place where chaos looks like order. The disorientation the labyrinth elicits helps explain why it is often perceived as a prison, an aporetic place where one "serves time," where time becomes unbearable, perhaps because one is so aware of its passing. Like the labyrinth, the prison historicizes the self (what Koerner calls the *Geschichtlichung des Selbst*), forces one to face one's own temporality. Koerner says that time is the central fact of the labyrinth, a fact that becomes manifest when you consider what lies at the labyrinth's center. In *Fors Clavigera,* Ruskin posits "that the question seems not at all to have been about getting in; but getting out again."[6] The desire of those who enter a labyrinth is to escape, and in one particular story, to escape the Minotaur that waits at the labyrinth's center. In the center of the labyrinth lies something timeless—death. For some reason, few have wondered about the Minotaur's desire to escape, but then another role of the labyrinth involves keeping horror in.

The labyrinth can be seen as a place of education, and it is typically imagined as a shadowy world. In fact, up until the nineteenth century, the Cretan labyrinth was often described as a cave, perhaps like the one in which Hermes was born.[7] In her essay on education, Hannah Arendt points out the need for darkness in pedagogy. She writes, "Children . . . require the security of concealment in order to mature undisturbed."[8] From her view, the school serves as buffer between the home and the world; in other words, "school in a sense represents the world, although it is not yet actually the world."[9] This complements the ancient role of labyrinths, which were used to initiate people.[10] What does one learn in a labyrinth? At least one answer that Arendt—not having labyrinths in mind—implicitly offers is that children learn that they must come to accept responsibility for a world they did not make. As with the fourteen sacrificial youths in one version of the Daedalus myth, the Athenian youths become implicated in an agreement between Minos and the Athenians that was probably made before many of the youths had been born. In this myth, the children become subject to agreements that they do not author themselves. These youths enter history *in medias res,* which means entering their own family's history as well as the history of the community in which they live, and emerging into laws and languages they had no part in shaping.

Arendt says that what prepares children for the world of adults is "the gradually acquired habit of work and of not-playing."[11] The word labyrinth is connected to labor.[12] What prepares children for the world of adults includes the ability to work their way through darkness. "To lose one's way in the dark pathways—that is the nightmare of the labyrinth," says Koerner.[13] Accepting the nightmarish lesson of the labyrinth—that you cannot return to the point from which you came—relates to the fact that you cannot turn around and go back into childhood when fear strikes, and that what awaits you at some point in your journey is something like the Minotaur, i.e., death.[14] Within the labyrinth, it compels you to consider your past—which you cannot fully retrace—your present confused state, and your future: the Minotaur. This is the historicizing of the self, for history leaves a trail like Ariadne's thread, which Theseus uses to make his way out, freeing himself through knowledge of the past and through another's love—an explanation of which you can find at the end of this chapter.

Until then, we can say that if nothing else, one makes many turns in a labyrinth, or rather the labyrinth turns one. You might take "turning" here in the sense of conversion, in Theseus's case a conversion from a youth into an adult. When Theseus leaves the labyrinth, he is perceived differently. To paraphrase Michel Foucault, the experience of the labyrinth metamorphoses those who enter. For those who enter, the labyrinth teaches them something about the way things are. Foucault: "At the most enigmatic moment, when all paths stop and when one is at the point of being lost, or at the absolute beginning, when one is on the threshold of something else, the labyrinth suddenly again offers the *same*."[15] Like an echo, the labyrinth repeats.

What does all this have to do with writing? It has come down to us from the past that Daedalus is an artist in a myth about art. In fact, in ancient Greece, artful works were called *daidala*. Artful works include labyrinths as well as labyrinthine texts—dark works filled with metaphors, puzzles, twists. The use of figurative language—tropes—involves turning; turning words, as Bruns would say, now this way now that, so that it becomes difficult to settle on a single understanding of a word or phrase, especially when the *same* word or phrase repeats itself in a different context. Repetition begins to look like something other than repetition. Echoes begin to take on histories.

We need to ruminate on the words associated with Daedalus, such as *daidalatos,* a work of art, and the verb *daidallo,* which means to work cunningly, curiously, to embellish; in the passive this verb means to be spotted or marked. In short, *daidallo* can be linked to constructions or art works that incorporate darkness. An example of a *daidalatos* is Borges's "Death and the Compass," a story that deals with labyrinths, and a character, a detective, who is compared to Auguste Dupin, viz., Erik Loennrot.[16] In this story, there are "symmetrical and periodic deaths," much like the ritual deaths of the Athenian youths in the Daedalus story. Let us place Loennrot in the role of Theseus, for like Theseus, Loennrot enters a labyrinth knowing that he will be killed. Although this story contains several labyrinths, Loennrot enters the one called the Triste-le-Roy, a villa that "abounded in pointless symmetries and in maniacal repetitions," a place of sameness, seemingly pointless sameness. Red Scharlach, the murderer, relates: "I felt that the world was a labyrinth, from which it was impossible to flee, for all roads, though they pretend to lead north or south, actually lead to Rome, which was also the quadrilateral jail where my brother was dying and the villa of Triste-le-Roy."[17] (Scharlach picks up the "all roads lead to Rome" phrase from a man who tried to *convert* him.) And, of course, Hermes is present, adding to the darkness. Although Loennrot enters the villa at dusk, "a two-faced Hermes projected a monstrous shadow." "Death and the Compass" mirrors "The Purloined Letter," not only in mentioning Dupin, but also in that Borges's tale, like Poe's, is one of revenge.

At the apparent end of this journey into a labyrinth, we find repeated an event familiar to the Athenian youths, but with a strange twist, an added repetition. Before Scharlach murders Loennrot, Loennrot mentions another kind of labyrinth: "I know of one Greek labyrinth which is a single straight line," and Loennrot requests that "when in some other incarnation" Scharlach seeks him out again, Scharlach should murder him in the labyrinth of the straight line. " 'The next time I kill you,' replies Scharlach, 'I promise you that labyrinth, consisting of a single line which is invisible and unceasing.' "[18] With this enigmatic dialogue ("The next time I kill you"), Borges introduces the notion of endless repetition.

II

Enter Gadamer, who, in one of his essays on writing ("*Unterwegs zur Schrift?*"), takes up the matter of repetition—particularly the repeating phrase—stressing the purpose of musical phrasings.[19] For instance, he directs our attention to the musical refrain, whose power lies "in the repetition and the familiar." The refrain helps the music to work its way into our memories, to become part of us, so that we might find ourselves unconsciously whistling a tune while walking. Gadamer says, "What is thoroughly didactic in this phenomenon of the phrase and the formalization of the recurrence of linguistic turnings is its suspension between bare execution and genuine stabilization of meaning."[20] In this quotation, Gadamer cites a relationship between repetition and learning, and "the connection [hanging together] between repetition, which is never entirely the same, and the constituting of one and the same." Gadamer uses the example of language acquisition to support his observation, noting that "the child learns the word, as it were, through repetitive speech attempts."[21]

When Gadamer shifts from speech to writing, he begins with a discussion of literary writing and with talk about inscriptions on graves (*Grabinschrift*), which serve the purpose of surviving in the memories of the living. The inscription maintains a fixity that exceeds mortality. Naturally, these grave inscriptions would include prayers and blessings, and in this essay about writing Gadamer tips the balance toward repetition's benefits in magical and personal affairs rather than repetition's formal, functional requirements. The word "Abracadabra" appeals to Gadamer more than a taxonomy of conventions of repetition.

As a Plato scholar, Gadamer cannot ignore the *Phaedrus* in an essay about writing. Gadamer views the *Phaedrus* as a dialogue about "the self-understanding of the passage from artful speech to artful prose."[22] While this strikes me as true, Martha Nussbaum's essay on the *Phaedrus* is a better aid here, for, amazingly, she seems to sidestep the matter of writing in the dialogue.[23] Moreover, the epigraph to this essay sums up almost all of her explicit commentary about writing in the *Phaedrus*. In place of a concentrated exegesis on writing in the dialogue, Nussbaum pursues the eroticism of discourse in both its written and spoken forms, thereby directing the reader to another kind of persuasion.

Contrasting two speeches in the dialogue, the first one modeled on the speech Lysias wrote for Phaedrus and the second delivered by an uncovered Socrates in slanted light, after the sun has reached its zenith, Nussbaum provides me with examples of what are taken for clear, straightforward writing and dark, slanted writing. That we are told these are speeches matters not for my task, since we read Plato's writing. Both speeches seek to persuade Phaedrus. Lysias desires Phaedrus, as does Socrates, but Nussbaum reveals how different these desires are, and how differently they manifest themselves.

From Nussbaum's perspective, Lysias's speech urges thorough self-possession, a subduing of emotion in favor of reason (*sophro-*

sune). Lysias wants Phaedrus to establish relations with someone (Lysias) who is not mad with erotic passion, who maintains a pure and clear intellect, and who can offer rational companionship. Regarding the style of Lysias's discourse, Nussbaum says, "We see his conception of objectivity in the spare, chaste prose style, pruned of every emotional indulgence, every appeal of feeling through metaphor and rhythm. The message of this style is that rationality is something crisp and cerebral, something of the *logistikon* alone."[24]

On the other hand, Socrates' speech after he uncovers himself endorses *mania* and an eroticism that is crucial to moral and philosophical development. In this uncovered speech, Socrates speaks of the soul's plumage and of a flood of passion. Rich, emotive, metaphorical, enfolded language comes into play. As Nussbaum says, it is a "moving and extraordinary description of passionate love." The power of this slanted speech moves Phaedrus, whereas the speech of Lysias set out not to arouse him. The criticism brought against Lysias is that despite all the purity and clarity, Lysias lacks *interest* in his subject.[25] Socrates shows interest in Phaedrus and tells Phaedrus about the pleasures and advantages of *mania,* which Nussbaum describes as follows:

> The life of *mania* is not the life of stable contemplation. Plato shows us that it would be safer to choose the closed, ascetic life of the *Phaedo*—or, not so different, the Lysian life of non-involved and painless sexuality. Stinginess is in general more stable than generosity, the closed safer than the open, the simple more harmonious than the complex. But he acknowledges that there are in this risky life (whose riskiness itself is made to seem rather splendid) sources of nourishment for the soul of a complex human being that are not found in any other type of philosophical life. He rejects the simplicity of the former ideal—and its associated conception of insight—in favor of a view of creativity and objectivity that expresses itself in imagery of flowing light and illuminated water, of plant growth, of movement and instability, reception and release.[26]

Now imagine a world in which most of the pupils are taught to write and think like Lysias—who have been told that the simple is more harmonious than the complex—and you will have imagined the context in which I propose a dark writing theory. In the next section, I will make the world of Ariadne and Phaedrus speak to the present.

III

Noted writer and Holocaust witness Elie Wiesel gave a speech a few years ago about language and its intricacies. To make his points, Wiesel often tells stories, such as the one he used to conclude his talk: "A Hasidic rabbi, known to be a seer, was called before the emperor, for the emperor wished to test the rabbi's abilities. 'Rabbi,' the emperor said, 'I have heard that you are a wise man. Let's see how wise you are. I am holding a bird behind my back, and I want you to tell me whether it is alive or dead.' The rabbi thought for a moment, and fearing that the emperor might kill the bird just to prove him wrong, he said, 'Your Majesty, the answer is in your hands.'"

Like a good rhetorician, the rabbi understands the *situation* he is in and acts accordingly. The rabbi cannot be clear in his response, nor can he remain silent, for the emperor has the political power in the situation. Using practical wisdom (*phronesis*), knowing how to act, the rabbi employs equivocation to retain his advantage, his power.

Put one of our students in the rabbi's position, and surely the bird would be killed. The student might not fare much better, not because the student would be a fool, but because the student would not have been instructed about such a situation. In the interests of clarity, which the student has been taught, the student would tell the emperor straightforwardly that he was not only evil, but an animal killer as well. As Richard Lanham says, most of our students are taught a variation of Lysian discourse, the C-B-S theory of writing: clarity, brevity, and sincerity, for we want, and expect, people to write prose that is clear, chaste, transparent.[27] Our textbooks on writing tell us always to be clear, that the best style is the never-noticed. We think people should be as literal as possible, for we associate literalness with honesty.

This seems to miss the point that whether something is clear, opaque, or otherwise depends in large part on the situation in which the words make their appearance, not on the words alone, for even the simplest words can have enormous depth to them. We might say that clarity is when at least one person in the process of conversation understands the other person. Language is always cryptic. J. L. Austin presents an example of some of the fine-tuning that can be done by contextualizing ordinary expressions. In "A Plea for Excuses," he writes, "We could scarcely hope for a more promising exercise than the study of excuses. Here, surely, is just the sort of situation where people will say 'almost anything,' because they are so flurried, or so anxious to get off. 'It was a mistake,' 'It was an accident.'" . . .[28] These expressions might seem to blur together until Austin sets them in the now-famous context:

> You have a donkey, so have I, and they graze in the same field. The day comes when I conceive a dislike for mine. I go to shoot it, draw a bead on it, fire: the brute falls in its tracks. I inspect the victim, and find to my horror that it is *your* donkey. I appear on your doorstep with the remains and say—what? 'I say, old sport, I'm awfully sorry, &c., I've shot your donkey *by accident*'? Or '*by mistake*'? Then again, I go to shoot my donkey as before, draw a bead on it, fire—but as I do so, the beasts move, and to my horror yours falls. Again the scene on the doorstep— what do I say? 'By mistake'? Or 'by accident'?[29]

What if we taught our students something that many people would call Machiavellian, that is, a dark writing theory, say a theory that taught people how to be equivocal, dialectical, ambiguous, to dissemble, to use what the Greeks called the *pseudos,* the false, that which masquerades as the true, or which can turn into the true when you are not looking? Can one know what the light is without ever having known darkness? What sort of human being knows how to construct labyrinthine prose? Emmanuel Levinas sums up what I am after here: "Another lesson in rhetoric. Indispensable in the struggle against the beguilements of the Devil: one must use the Devil's own tools."[30]

We fail to teach our students the history of writing and the politics of writing, and we instruct them to be as limpid as possible without letting them know that such transparency gives others control over them, as if they were safely enclosed in a classroom with walls of one-way mirrors; they can be seen, but the students cannot see who is observing and controlling them. Caveat: This is not an argument against the authority of the teacher, nor a sweeping gesture against authority of all kinds. Arendt makes a convincing case on this matter:

> By being emancipated from the authority of adults [in so-called non-authoritarian classrooms] the child has not been freed but has been subjected to a much more terrifying and truly tyrannical authority, the tyranny of the majority. In any case the result is that the children have been so to speak banished from the world of grown-ups. They are either thrown back upon themselves or handed over to the tyranny of their own group, against which, because of its numerical superiority, they cannot rebel. . . .
>
> Education can play no part in politics, because in politics we always have to deal with those who are already educated. . . . He who seriously wants to create a new political order through education, that is, neither through force and constraint nor through persuasion, must draw the dreadful Platonic conclusion: the banishment of all older people from the state that is to be founded.[31]

Our students need to know that lucidity has social as well as personal consequences, that there have been times in history when people have not been able to write plainly (as if such a thing were possible), nor to speak plainly—when, in fact, it would have been foolish to do so, if one wanted to live. It is no coincidence that the Greek verb *graphein* means both to write and to indict. Isn't writing a way of informing others about ourselves? By writing, are we not informants on ourselves? As Machiavelli says in a chapter called "On Conspiracies" in his *Discourses:* "Nothing is more likely to convict you than your own handwriting."[32]

Insofar as I am stressing the importance of historical awareness, as well as situational awareness, let me offer an example, a story, taken from Carlo Ginzburg's *The Cheese and the Worms*. Ginzburg recounts the tale of a sixteenth-century miller who believed that God and the angels came from the material universe the way worms come from cheese. The miller's name was Menocchio, a man known by the other villagers to speak his mind, to be straightforward. He offers such opinions as: "Priests want us under their thumb, just to keep us quiet, while they have a good time"; "I say that it is a greater rule to love one's neighbor than to love God"; "I think speaking Latin is a betrayal of the poor, because in lawsuits the poor do not know what is being said and are crushed, and if they want to say four words, they need a lawyer"; "I do believe that every person considers his faith to be right, and we do not know which is the right one."[33] As Ginzburg tells us:

> Menocchio was proudly aware of the originality of his ideas: because of this he wanted to expound them to the highest religious and secular authorities. But at the same time he felt the need to master the culture of his adversaries. He understood that the written word, and the ability to master and to transmit written culture, were sources of power, so he didn't confine himself to denouncing a "betrayal of the poor" in the use of bureaucratic (and sacerdotal) language such as Latin. The scope of his polemic was broader. "Can't you understand," Menocchio said, "the inquisitors don't want us to know what they know!" (P. 59)

This diaphanous discourse naturally displeased the authorities, and Menocchio was brought to trial in 1584. Yet, at the trial, the inquisitors did not discourage clarity, but—like modern-day writing teachers—insisted on it. One of the inquisitors said, "So, tell the truth and speak more openly than you did in the preceding examination" (p. 71). Later, after his second trial in 1599, Menocchio's son warns him that his clarity is getting him in trouble, and that if Menocchio must use clarity, he should use it to try to appease those in power. Thus, Menocchio writes in a letter in which he tries to persuade his inquisitors that he is innocent: "It is indeed true that I thought and believed and said, as appears in the trial records, things against the commandments of God and the Holy Church. I said them through the will of the false spirit who blinded my intellect and memory and will, making me think, believe, and say what was false and not true, and so I confess that I thought and believed and said what was false and not true and so I gave my opinion but I did not say that it was the truth" (p. 87). (Even in the translation there is a distinction between what is false and what is not true; they are not synonymous.) "I do not want to think or believe except what the

Holy Church believes and to do what my priests and superiors will command of me" (p. 109). Menocchio misunderstands the situation. While he thinks he is engaged in a dialogue about theological matters with people who consider him an equal, he is not in a dialogue at all, but in a situation in which his interlocutors are scrutinizing his discourse. Inquisition is not dialogue. Thus Menocchio's glassy text, as clear as the best student paper, succeeds; he reveals to the authorities that he is guilty, and in 1599, by order of the Holy Office, Domenico Scandella, called Menocchio, was burned at the stake.

Curious that Menocchio's name is Scandella, for he is a scandal, which derives from the Greek *skandalon,* a snare, which is what Menocchio ends up in, a snare, a fix. His words come back to haunt him, not necessarily because he spoke them, but because during his trials, his words were set down in writing. A permanent member of every inquisitorial court was the notary, who transcribed as the legal manuals required "not only all the defendant's responses and any statements he might make, but also what he might utter during torture, even his sighs, his cries, his laments and tears."[34] Thus Menocchio's scandalous words shine forth from the trial record as if the document were a damning illuminated manuscript. Once his words could be gone over again in writing, contradictions, errors, and heresies appeared.

To us, perhaps, what Menocchio said is true, but to the inquisitors, Menocchio's words appeared in a different light, were put in a different context. Menocchio could not fix his words as he tried to do in his letter to the inquisitors; rather, his words got away from him, fell into the wrong hands. His discourse was inappropriate to the situation in which he found himself. Perhaps Menocchio did not understand the nature of the letter. We are still not comfortable with the ancients' view of language, for they understood that writing is an estrangement, a separating of the word from the person, a kind of alienation. This is what Plato talks about in the *Phaedrus.* For Socrates, writing is an act whose secrecy is irreversible, and he worried about what would happen if words fell into uncomprehending hands, since writing cannot speak for itself. As we have seen, writing is defenseless against misinterpretation. Without any chameleon-like potential, writing slides unchanged into new situations.

Like Socrates, some of us might become extremely suspicious of writing and language, given this seeming madness of words, their ability to slip from our grasp, to turn this way and that, meaning now one thing, and a moment later—in a different context, before a different audience—another. Like Socrates, we want to anchor our words, bind them through definition, for definition finalizes meaning; we want to literalize words so that they will always mean what they say, and for which history and context will be irrelevant. We might call this the desire to systematize, to order, to bring under control.

The *hermeneus* (the ancient term for one who is skilled in dealing with texts) revels in the looseness of language, in language's open-endedness, its wiliness, its way of slipping out from under definition before it can be pinned down. The *hermeneus* and the rhetor would find closer kinship with Odysseus than with Saussure or with linguists and grammarians. Surely, Odysseus does not get pinned down, for he is cunning with his speech. Think of his meeting with Polyphemous. Polyphemous cannot cope with the polysemous.

Ambiguity and darkness of language can produce the indeterminacy that allows for richness of meaning and multiplicity, so that texts always have something to say to the present while at the same time teaching us about the past.[35] This outlook runs counter to the search for certitude that accompanies Cartesian Anxiety, though even shortly after Descartes's time, rhetoricians spoke up against constricting methodologies and certitude. Giambattista Vico, who held the Chair of Rhetoric at the University of Naples in the early part of the eighteenth century, said:

> Since the sole aim of study today is truth, we investigate the nature of things, because this seems certain, but not the nature of people, because free will makes this extremely uncertain. This method of study gives rise to the following disadvantages for people: that later they neither engage in public life with enough wisdom, nor know sufficiently well how to imbue oratory with morality and inflame it with feeling. . . . [Recall

Socrates' inflamed speech to Phaedrus.] Those whose only concern is for the truth find it difficult to attain the means, and even more the ends of public life. More often than not they give up, frustrated in their own plans and deceived by those of others.[36]

The ancient *hermeneus* understood the political nature of writing and saw potential meaning in everything, even in the way letters were formed. This sounds like an oddity, but Stanley Morison's *Politics and Script,* a book about the history of letter formation, reminds us that the ordering of writing was and is indeed ordered. For instance, "The contrasted and serified letters we now call 'Roman' begin to appear with the genesis of the imperial power which made them its symbol."[37] This is approximately the time of Julius Caesar's reign. Later, Constantine, a Christian emperor of the fourth century A.D. brought about other changes in script: "The destruction of the Christian libraries by Diocletian required, under the new regime, wholesale reconditioning and replenishment. . . . For writing this mass of new books the appropriate script would clearly not be one closely associated with the persecutors. . . . The new day was the day of the Evangelists, the theologians, fathers and Apologists. These of course had written in Greek."[38] Thus a handwriting similar to old Greek was devised. Morison follows the history of the written word to our own century, showing that the political connection to letter formation is not peculiar to ancient times. For example, cursive writing came into use, in part, for economic reasons; businessmen needed to conduct financial affairs quickly, so they required a kind of writing that would allow for increased speed.

Still, for the *hermeneus,* knowing the formation of the letters would not be enough, because one could encounter a text like Maimonides' (1135–1204) *Guide for the Perplexed,* which appears to be Hebrew. But Maimonides was a crafty fellow like Odysseus; in order to prevent his text from falling into unfaithful hands, he wrote the text in Arabic, but used Hebrew characters.[39] Texts like this are often produced not out of playfulness, but out of the author's fear of persecution, out of an intense awareness of circumstances. In Leo Strauss's important essay, "Persecution and the Art of Writing," he says, "Persecution . . . gives rise to a peculiar technique of writing, and therewith to a peculiar type of literature, in which the truth about all crucial things is presented exclusively between the lines."[40] Notice that moderns think dark writing arises out of fear.

Imagine a student brought up in the C-B-S way of life encountering *The Guide for the Perplexed* or the "peculiar" literature of which Strauss writes. Such works would leave the student baffled. Here you might object that no student you have ever known has looked at Maimonides' text. But students do come across similarly alien texts—e.g., allegories—though students are rarely told to look beyond the surface of an allegory like *The Wizard of Oz,* for instance. Most people see the Oz tales as simple children's entertainment, but people like Stewart Robb, writing for *New Masses* in 1938, view the Oz tales as allegories that can be activated for political purposes.[41] For some, seeing politics in the Oz series is as incomprehensible as the fact that the Dies committee once accused Shirley Temple of being a Communist.

It is important for students to study texts like allegories, because a literal understanding of an allegory would miss the whole point. How does a student trained in clarity deal with protean prose or a dark text, one that withholds its secrets, yet draws the reader in with its thaumaturgical qualities? The study of rhetoric and hermeneutics, both of which entail the study of the history of such things as interpretation, writing, and politics, could help students to live in what William James calls "the pluralistic universe"—or in a world that gives the appearance of being pluralistic; it could help them to learn to take things now this way, now that, in the fashion of dialogue and dialectic. Students could be taught how to assess various situations and what sort of discourses might work with what audiences. Like the Greek sophists, students could become masters of the *dissoi logoi,* the dexterity for arguing many sides of a matter. And they could become at least apprentices of the magical art of writing we can call *skiagraphia,* shadow writing, the sort of writing one would have to do in a labyrinth.[42] Finally, the students might come to understand dialectic the way Gadamer does. In an essay on "Dialectic and Sophism in Plato's *Seventh Letter,*" Gadamer observes that for Plato, dialectic is not a method or systematic construction but a condition of understanding in which one is never able to achieve single-mindedness or dogmatism. In Plato's *Sophist,* for example, Gadamer says dialectic

> results from the multiplicity of respects in which something may be interpreted in language. In this regard one might be reminded of the first hypothesis in the *Parmenides*. There that multiplicity was not a burdensome ambiguity to be eliminated but an entirety of interrelated aspects of meaning which articulate a field of knowing. The multiple valences of meaning which separate from one another in speaking about things contain a productive ambiguity. . . . The productivity of this dialectic is the positive side of the ineradicable weakness from which the procedure of conceptual determination suffers. That ever-contemporary encounter with the logoi of which Plato speaks is found here in its most extreme form. It is displayed here as the experience which we have when the conventional meaning of single words gets away from us. But Plato knows full well that his source of aporia ["being at a loss"] is also the source of euporia ["insight"] which we achieve in discourse. He who does not want the one will have to do without the other.[43]

This is followed by Gadamer's famous statement that the whole basis of language is metaphor, a good example of which is Lenin's 1921 speech "Once Again on the Trade Unions." In this speech, Lenin attempts to counter some arguments of Trotsky and Bukharin and to demonstrate Marxist dialectic by offering the various perspectives one can have of a tumbler.[44] Dialectic has this tumbling, gathering quality that makes full use of the *copia*. This so-on-and-so-forth attitude makes one see that matters are not black and white, but continually changing, as contexts and situations change. However, continual changes might also be changes that are made in order to keep things the same, to keep people under control, and this constitutes the modern fear of authoritarianism.

We ask our students to put down their thoughts—not pick them up to use them—in a black-and-white fashion, believing that black and white correspond to simplicity, that plainness is somehow closer to truth and goodness. Yet, our students do not live in a world that is black and white.

This equation—that plainness equals goodness—carries over into our lives in activities like shopping and in our notions about "generic" products, which are counterparts to "good" student papers—unadorned, simple, straightforward, devoid of anything that smacks of subtlety, slyness, or interest, since teachers reward objectivity. Most of us think that generic products are cheaper, because the companies save on expensive colored packaging that is designed to deceive us anyway. As Milton Glaser points out, "The truth of the matter is that generic packaging costs exactly the same to produce as conventional. The fact that you do not use many colors does not mean a thing."[45] Glaser works for the Grand Union supermarket chain which began a line of generic goods called "Basics." A client of Glaser's decided that his supermarket must also look generic, so the client took over an old market and spent $50,000 ripping up the perfectly good old tile floor, because "one of the signals that it is not a fancy place is that you have a concrete floor." Glaser says, "Generic marketing is a response to the kind of calculating consumer who knows he [sic] does not need the fancier stuff and thinks he is able to read through the myths of advertising." Even a marketplace without designs has designs on us.

Part of the reason people like Glaser can know so much about customers is this one-way system into which each of us is plugged. Robert Smith, publisher of *Privacy Journal,* says: "Each American citizen appears, on the average, in 18 different federal data bases. We are also logged on 16 state and six local data bases. And each of us appears in around 25 different data bases in the private sector."[46] If people in power want to find out about you, all they need do is consult the system. You, on the other hand, are kept in the dark about what the authorities are up to. It is quite difficult to uncover what the powerful are doing because, among other things, they employ cryptography in their communication—perhaps because these people know that few could cope with language that is not what it seems. (Cryptography is from the Greek *kryptos* [hidden] and *graphein* [to write].) Since ancient times, military and government officials have exchanged information in this dark way. Ralph Weber, author of a book on diplomatic codes used in the United States since the time of the Revolutionary War, notes that while government officials seek to tighten security through more cryptology research, research that makes Maimonides' efforts at concealment look, at best, elementary, they also look for new ways to violate the privacy of citizens. For example: "Apparently since 1927, cables sent through the British Post Office and through foreign cable companies were handed over to security officials on a daily basis. In September 1976, it was revealed that Western Union International prepared copies of all private cables to the U.S. and submitted them to British security officers. Similarly, American international telegraph companies reportedly gave copies of private cable communications to the National Security Agency."[47] This is one way of bringing things to light, as is going through a secretary's wastebasket and finding a used carbon ribbon. Everything that was written is there—only backwards. Of course, these methods are crude in our world of spy satellites, laser monitoring systems, and computers.

IV

Clearly, suspicion fills the descriptions I have given of the situation students find themselves in, and we are a long way from the story of Daedalus and Phaedrus. Most of the examples presented above assuage those who fear authority, but they also show that authority, like anything else, can go bad; the examples are true enough. Still, fear of authority and fear in general are precisely the problems with education, including the teaching of writing. We can return to Hannah Arendt, who observes: "Authority has been discarded by the adults, and this can mean only one thing: that the adults refuse to assume responsibility for the world into which they have brought the children."[48] The failure to assume responsibility, like a Lysian prose style, comes from a failure to love. "Education is the point at which we decide whether we love the world enough to assume responsibility for it."[49] Given the present situation with education, Nussbaum's interpretation of the *Phaedrus* takes on more significance for those who want to think through what it means to write and to read. By concentrating on love, on the erotic side of persuasion, Nussbaum impresses on us a view of what education can be like once trust replaces suspicion, or once subjectivity (interest in another) overcomes objectivity. When trust abounds, the use of a plain style will not seem out of place. When suspicion abounds, a plain style leaves its user exposed.

Arendt says that "the function of the school is to teach children what the world is like." The world is like a labyrinth. You can perceive that labyrinth as a prison, as a place of death, or as a place of education where love is present along with death, which is my reading of the Daedalus story. Some confirmation of this can be found in Ruskin's translation of an inscription beside a labyrinth on the southern wall of the porch of the Cathedral of Lucca:

> This is the labyrinth which the Cretan Dedalus built,
> Out of which nobody could get who was inside,
> Except Theseus; nor could he have done it,
> unless he had been helped with a thread by Ariadne,
> all of love.[50]

$\mathcal{P}$ostmodernism, Allegory, and Hermeneutics in *Brazil*

Postmodernism tends to substitute enactment for interpretation—a rhetorical approach for the acknowledgment of history—tends to project a two-dimensional world in which line is freed from contour; narrative movement is lateral rather than progressive; figures, even objects are not depicted. . . . Postmodern describes a sensibility, a feeling for innovation, for experiment with conventional ways of framing experience so that it is at once removed from recognizable relationships and from the locations in which they exist. This movement is variously informed by a skeptical attitude toward illusion, toward a recognizable psychology of human relationships, and toward coherence of any sequence of actions.—Stanley Trachtenberg, *The Postmodern Moment*

Where everything is bad it must be good to know the worst.
—F. H. Bradley

The almost insoluble task is to let neither the power of others, nor our own powerlessness stupefy us.—Theodor Adorno, *Minima Moralia*

This chapter presents a version of a response to a question posed by the film *Brazil:* What does it mean to try to understand what claims to be aporetic, where aporetic means not that ways of understanding cannot be found, but that a hundred roads diverge in a tangled wood, inviting dispersion?

For the hermeneuticist, *aporiai* are invitations to possible insight. Whereas some see aporetic texts as sources of confusion and bewilderment, a hermeneuticist like Gadamer views confusion and bewilderment as nascent stages on the way to understanding and self-understanding. Conundrums and puzzles lead us to think. Gadamer writes, "It is invariably true that when we see something we must think of something in order to see anything."[1] Resistance to interpretation provokes, but Gadamer does not take this provocation as a belligerent act, rather as a condition of life, a life in which "we proceed constantly through the coexistence of past and future," through the familiar and the strange. "The essence of spirit lies in the ability to move within the horizon of an open future and an unrepeatable past."[2] To engage in this movement requires stepping out of one's complacency, for as Gerald Bruns explains, "The end of hermeneutical experience is not meaning or knowledge but openness, where openness, however, does not mean simply open-mindedness, or tolerance for another's views, the mutual indulgence of liberal pluralists [or postmodernists], but rather acknowledgment of what is alien and refractory to one's categories. It means acknowledging the being of what refuses to fit or refuses to be known, that which says 'no' to me."[3]

A meeting with something or someone aporetic calls us to do something. Of course, some practitioners of the hermeneutics of suspicion will say an interpretation of the different constitutes a form of co-option or assimilation that wipes out difference. However, Gadamer's discussion of our experience with strangeness—particularly with art—insists on "allowing what is to be."[4] We must allow the work of art, the strangeness (whatever form it might take), to speak to us, and "we must realize that every work of art only begins to speak when we have already learned to decipher it."[5] Strangeness and otherness acquire meaning in relation to our ability to take it upon ourselves to produce a shared community of meaning.

My task here with *Brazil* involves discovering what can be said about the film, perhaps producing possible meanings worked out in view of the situation at hand, viz., postmodernism. I am appropriating *Brazil* to make it speak to present debates about postmodernism, and I do not feign neutrality in these debates. Be sure to note my use of rhetoric in this chapter, a type of rhetoric that "freely asserts that it will assume what it needs in order to preserve a case it deems worth making."[6] I will concentrate on plausible readings of the film, using as much material evidence as possible, while making a case for the architectural side of postmodernism with its emphasis on rhetoric as civic argument, and on historical awareness.

I

To call *Brazil* "postmodern" is to open myself to attack by Socrates-like people who demand the rigor of definition, because what is to be called postmodern is still under debate. Postmodernism has yet to petrify, even though many are ready to label it "regressive" (Habermas, Jameson), others "progressive" (Ulmer, Rapaport). The practices of postmodernism are diverse (and perhaps diversionary). It refers to a multiplicity of cultural practices characterized by such things as collage, hybridization, distortion of scale, pastiche, and unreadability. More generally, postmodernism might be called the new Rococo. Etymologically, rococo is a word that means the fanciful alteration of *rocaille* shellwork. As its critics stress, this etymology presents a major problem in postmodernism, that is, that postmodernism functions as a shell without any substance, that the postmodern is but a play of surfaces, like a Hollywood set composed entirely of façades, or like the hydrodynamics of a soap bubble. Critics might call it ornamentation without foundation, without purpose. The postmodern shell covers a void.[7]

Although the word "postmodernism" appears as early as 1934 in Federico de Onis's *Antologia de la poesia espanola e hispanoamericana,*[8] postmodernism comes into its own through architecture, and the postmodern movement in architecture becomes associated with architects like Gae Aulenti, Robert Venturi, Charles Jencks, and Paolo Portoghesi. The beginnings of Postmodernism in architecture are quite different from the postmodernism Habermas or Jameson talk about. For instance, Venturi's *Complexity and Contradiction in Architecture* (1966) suggests not ahistoricism but historical awareness, not incoherence but intricacy and ambiguity. Venturi reacts against modernism and its "clean," "straightforward," "articulated," "pure" structures. Venturi says, "I am for messy vitality over obvious unity. I include the non sequitur and proclaim the duality."⁹ Still, these non sequiturs and dualities are not meant to banish readability or truth. "A valid architecture," he says, "evokes many levels of meaning and combinations of focus: its space and its elements become readable and workable in several ways at once."¹⁰ Venturi sounds much like Paul Ricoeur, who in *Interpretation Theory* says that metaphors and complexities within a sentence do not undo meaning, but offer a reader a surplus of meaning. In *Architecture Today,* Charles Jencks echoes the notion of surplus meaning: "A Post-Modern building is double coded—part Modern and something else: vernacular, revivalist, local, commercial, metaphorical, or contextual. In several important instances it is also double coded in the sense that it seeks to speak on two levels at once [the allegorical side of postmodern architecture]: to a concerned minority of architects, an elite who recognize the subtle distinctions of a fast-changing language, and to the inhabitants, users, or passersby, who want only to understand and enjoy it."¹¹ The use of language in Jencks's description suggests what could be called a rhetorical architecture, for it is concerned with context and audience, with delighting or persuading an audience, much in the manner of a sophist trying to win over a crowd. Think of sophists as Brian Vickers does, as people devoted to the practicalities of civic life.¹² Rhetorical architecture commands the attention of those capable of being initiated into what is hidden, or double coded, those who want to see more. The complexity of architecture teaches the inhabitants that there is something *more* to be understood.

The rhetorical side of early postmodern architecture emerges most clearly in the work of Paolo Portoghesi, who, in what Jencks calls "his most creative book," *The Rome of Borromini: Architecture as a Language* (1967), showed that Borromini "used a highly rhetorical set of figures and complex language, because he was strongly motivated to communicate specific religious and structural ideas to a wide audience and to sustain interest in, and continual reinterpretation of, these ideas."¹³ Portoghesi's own work and writings reflect his interest in Borromini, in the value of communication and continual interpretation, which shows an awareness of Gadamer's point in *Truth and Method*—that we are always understanding differently. To plagiarize from Bruns: the pleroma, the fullness of time, will bring out the plethora of meaning.

Unlike some postmodernists, Portoghesi does not wish to erase history and tradition. In fact, the theme of the 1980 Venice Biennale (Portoghesi was the organizer of the architecture section of the Biennale), where postmodern architecture came into public prominence, was "The Presence of the Past." John Blatteau elaborated on the theme in his architectural self-portrait for the exhibition: "It is again possible to learn from tradition and to connect one's work with the fine and beautiful works of the past."[14] Clearly, these architects listen to what has come down from the past, and the hope is to make the past present again, to appropriate the past for present use, to see the present as a present the people of the past have given us. In short, Portoghesi's postmodernism is not out to absence presence. One of the characteristics of postmodernist architects is their effort to construct buildings that "echo" features of nearby buildings, making this sort of architecture a manifestation of heteroglossia, as if the structure were a combination of voices.

While it is not homogeneous, postmodernism in architecture, for the most part, differs greatly from many other manifestations of postmodernism, and I cannot account for this difference. When postmodernism leaves architecture and enters the discourse of literary criticism and philosophy, it takes a nasty negative turn and becomes a conglomerative carnival of cacophony, assimilating extremely heterogeneous modes of stylistic expression. But often this expression aims not to press out, or make its way out to others; instead, postmodernist expression in its nonarchitectural context seeks to excommunicate, to cut people off from a common base of understanding. Naturally, exceptions exist, notably Barbara Kruger and Hans Haacke, among others. Not to understand becomes one of the goals of postmodernism; or, at least, postmodernists like to frustrate or "problematize" understanding. Derrida's method of using paronomasia in his works serves as an example of this postmodernist strategy to move away from any grounding—in other words, to float. Those who float do not take up any position in the sense of a stand. The acceptance of neutrality in this version of postmodernism turns against rhetoric, against *peitho*. To be persuaded of something—the design the rhetorician has on an audience—is to take a position (perhaps even a dance position, and human dance requires a ground; one submits to the hegemony of gravity). As we will discover, rhetoric is far more than persuasion.

From another perspective, postmodernism's attraction to the performative could be seen as a prerhetorical, or protorhetorical moment, as one of the few ways expression can make its way in the world in the face of a crushing hegemony. According to one account of the origin of rhetoric, Sicily in 467–466 B.C. was ruled by two tyrants, Gelon and Hieron. "It is said that the tyrants indulged their savagery to the extent of forbidding the Syracusans to utter and sound at all but to signify what was appropriate by means of their feet, hands, and eyes whenever one of them was in need. It was in this way, they say, that dance-pantomime [*orchestike*] had its beginnings. Because the Syracusans had been cut off from speech, they contrived to explain their business with gestures [or dance-figures: *schemansi*]."[15] As part of the commentary on this passage, Vincent Farenga says, "Rhetoric is not, then, innate to human society, but it nonetheless comes to the citizens as something they need to regain their self-presence, their identity or true nature."[16]

Dance, which one might also see as a form of play—and as something not confined to aesthetics, as the Syracusans could attest—links us with identity, presence, ground. It is play in the way Gadamer speaks of it, in the way he appeals to the original meaning of play (*Spiel*) as dance. "The movement which is play," Gadamer says, "has no goal which brings it to an end; rather it renews itself in constant repetition."[17] This conception of play and repetition differs greatly from that of postmodernists like Derrida, who employs repetition to reveal the negativity in play. Gadamer also notes that subjectivity dissolves in play, for it is play playing, but the play leads to the player's reconciliation with self: "That which detaches [the player] from everything also gives him back the whole of his being."[18]

From the side of postmodernism, play empties being. Despite

feeling trapped and tyrannized, postmodernists still dance. Derrida, for instance, wishes to expunge presence and identity through a certain kind of play—frivolity. "Philosophical style congenitally leads to frivolity," he writes. "If philosophical writing is frivolous, that is because the philosopher cannot fulfill his statements. He knows nothing, he has nothing to say, and he complicates, subtilizes, refines the stylistic effects to mask his ignorance [masks will become important in the discussion of *Brazil*]. Thus he misleads, pays change out of the essential emptiness of his discourse."[19] Hans Blumenberg understands the relationship between this negativity and frivolity, and his perspective unsettles Derrida's playfulness: "One who discovers the law of increasing misery sees everything driving toward a point at which the only thing left is for everything to become different [*différance*]. Frivolity is only a weak derivative of all this, a means of anthropomorphic relaxation of tension vis-à-vis myth: One can do this, or say that, without being struck by lightning. It is the first stage of 'Enlightenment' satire, of rhetorical secularization as a stylistic technique employed by a spirit that is not yet confident of its [or his] enlightened status."[20] This links up with Stanley Rosen's claim that postmodernism is not an attack on Enlightenment, but rather its continuation. Derrida claims that frivolity begins its work in repetition, "in the fissure which, separating two repetitions, rends repetition in two. The repetition of the idea, the identity of ideas is not frivolous. Identity in words is frivolous."[21] The repetition of words characterizes Derrida's writing, for he wishes to show how supplementarity is at work. Repeating a word places it in a new context, giving it a different sense. The infinity of contexts in which words appear eliminates the possibility of words having univocal meanings, or what might be called an identity. This is what Derrida calls iterability. Part of Derrida's project involves exacerbating this iterability to produce undecidability. He empties language by overfilling it with frivolity, but decorating the margins to make a kind of illuminated manuscript that gives off no light, only lightness. This frivolity, however, is not to be taken frivolously. Derrida can do willful violence with deconstruction, for he can use repetition in its etymological sense, i.e., to attack again. Then again, one might see, as Richard Bernstein has begun to, that even deconstruction is done in the name of something.[22] As Maurice Blanchot says of Mallarmé's work: "As if in nothingness there were a strange power of affirmation."[23]

It becomes clear that Gadamer's and Derrida's notion of play, or frivolity, are different. One point that distinguishes Gadamer's talk of play from postmodern play is that Gadamer's play looks like children's play. In *Truth and Method,* for instance, he talks about the children's game of "Tinker, Tailor, Soldier, Sailor," and the way children play motor-cars.[24] On the other hand, postmodern play is sophisticated adult play that often is not play at all, but overly self-conscious self-consciousness, which continually denies itself. It plays off a self-lesser-than-thou attitude.

Bernstein refers to postmodernism in its literary and philosophical manifestations as the New Skepticism. Postmodernism feeds on suspicion. As Ihab Hassan writes, "The postmodernist only disconnects; fragments are all he pretends to trust."[25] In its classical sense, rhetoric connects disconnected parties, brings together fragments, and stabilizes a situation, not to fashion an oppressive totality—the great fear of postmodernists—but to work out an agreement for the common good. Brian Vickers says the ancients had a "conception of rhetoric as public debate in a society guaranteeing free speech, a debate in which both sides [perhaps more] of the case are heard and those qualified to vote come to a decision binding on parties."[26]

And this is why I choose to stay with the side of rhetoric rather than postmodernism, because rhetoric signals a return to civic matters, to a need to work and talk with others, to trust (wobbly as that trust might be), where trust means acknowledging heterogeneity, the conflicts of individuals and groups, as well as aiming for some common good. Rhetoric makes its full appearance in the "original" story of rhetoric with the entrance of Korax, who, after the Syracusans overthrow the tyrants, steps forward when everyone is talking and persuades the crowd to be silent. Korax transforms democratic noise into silence again, but this silence comes about through *peitho* rather than *bia,* consent rather than compulsion. If anything is to be said, there must be some stability, and it becomes the rhetorician's task to establish a situation in which someone can speak and be heard. Some postmodernists will assert that this stabilizing constitutes a suppression of voices, and they will be right. Gerald Bruns sums up this account of rhetoric's beginnings by saying, "The whole lesson of rhetoric, it turns out, is not how to speak, but how to render others speechless. . . . Rhetoric is the recuperation of tyranny by means of language."[27] Rhetoric also has its dark side, which must be acknowledged and understood. However, objections to rhetoric emerge from a view that ties power only to speaking, whereas Gadamer reminds us of the power of the ear in its resistance to suppression. "It is not just that he who hears is also addressed, but also that he who is addressed must hear whether he wants to or not. When you look at something, you can also look away from it by looking in another direction, but you cannot 'hear away.' "[28]

II

A facet of postmodernism that requires attention, in relation to *Brazil,* is the turn toward allegory. Long disparaged, allegory re-emerges as an important part of postmodernism, without its Christian cross to bear, without much weight at all in the case of *Brazil.* In a two-part article, Craig Owens speaks of an "allegorical impulse" in postmodernism.[29] Why this impulse? In "Notes on the Reemergence of Allegory," Stephen Melville says we live in "an age whose relation to its past has become problematic. . . . [This age] will be led to find and guarantee itself and its work through detour and delay—works and devices of indirection."[30] Allegory is indirect discourse, a speaking otherwise. As Gadamer says, " 'Allegory' originally belonged to the sphere of talk, of the logos, and is therefore a rhetorical and hermeneutical figure. Instead of what is actually meant, something else, more tangible, is said, but in such a way that the former is understood."[31] In other words, allegory points to a condition in which what needs to be said cannot be said directly for some reason. Some, like Lukacs, have looked negatively on allegory because of its indirection. Lukacs tells us that "allegory is the aesthetic genre which lends itself par excellence to a description of man's alienation from objective reality. Allegory is a problematic genre because it rejects the assumption of an immanent meaning to human existence."[32] Given that allegory presupposes mass access to several "levels" of meaning, I do not think allegory is divisive and alienating as Lukacs makes it out to be. On the contrary, allegory, as Bruns figures it, protects us. The truth cannot be viewed directly, so allegory, or "the veil of words," mediates the truth. Without the curtain or the veil, we would be unable to see anything at all, because the light would blind us. Bruns writes: "No doubt it is the job of understanding to penetrate the veil of words and to disclose what is hidden, but in fact the understanding cannot accomplish the task quite in this way. He who understands something is usually less knowledgeable than resourceful. He is able to regard what is hidden by constructing a version of it or by construing a meaning of what is not evident—but throughout all of his artfulness the veil remains intact."[33] The reader does not pass over the surface of the allegory, for the surface gives what is to be understood. It is not surprising, then, that the surfaces of allegories are detailed, ornamented, specific in a very odd way, since the extreme specificity provides clues to general insights, to larger cultural associations. In its simplistic form, allegory toys with generality, as in the case of the medieval play *Everyman,* in which the characters' names reveal their roles in the drama. In the modern and postmodern periods, allegories tend to be less like *Everyman* and more like Kafka's stories, say, "In the Penal Colony." Although this modernist text assigns characters general names like the Officer and the Explorer (making it similar to the *Everyman* allegory), Kafka includes a far more intricate allegorical surface in, for example, his complex description of the machine used for punishment. In the tale, the Officer tries to help the Explorer understand the machine by showing him the plans for the device. "The Explorer would have liked to say something appreciative, but all he could see was a labyrinth of lines crossing and recrossing each other, which covered the paper so thickly that it was difficult to discern the blank spaces between them."[34] Despite the opacity of the text before him, the Explorer realizes that there is something to be understood, but as an outsider, as one who is uninitiated, he is not prepared to understand. For the moment, then, he is unable to read what is going on, so he is stopped at the surface. My question about *Brazil* is related to the Explorer's dilemma: What happens to understanding when all is surface? What happens when a veil conceals nothing?

Like Kafka's allegories, *Brazil* presents a detailed elaborate surface. At the beginning of the film, the time and approximate historical period appear on the screen. It is 8:49 p.m.; the action takes place "Somewhere in the 20th Century." These two items reveal themselves to be pseudo-details, allegorical touches without allegorical import. The time is a needlessly precise detail; on the other hand, the tag "Somewhere in the 20th Century" constitutes an overly generalized piece of information, like the *Everyman* title. *Brazil* quickly moves to contradict this generality, for the film shows the viewer a chronologically specific world of cars, computers, televisions, microwave ovens—a world familiar to the middle class of an advanced industrial society. The effect is something like the Russian formalist notion of *ostrananie,* the device of making something familiar strange in order that the viewer or reader might see the familiar as if for the first time. For instance, the computers in the film look like the computers now in use, except the keyboards have the kind of keys one would find on an old manual typewriter, and the monitor, instead of being a box like a television set, is more like a thick piece of glass. The disguising, or the allegorizing here, is of the slimmest sort, so that the boundaries between reality and allegory dissolve. In other words, reality does not seem to buttress the disguise, as if there were no face to support the mask.

"Allegory," says Craig Owens, "is consistently attracted to the fragmentary, the imperfect, the incomplete—an affinity which finds its most comprehensive expression in the ruin. . . ."[35] *Brazil's* ruin is Sam Lowry. He is fragmented, imperfect, and incomplete—Postmodern Man. "Ruin" is from the Latin verb "to fall," which is what happens to Sam from the outset: His course is steadily downward. One can even find the word "low" in his name.

The first time we see Sam, we do not see Sam, but rather his

heroic vision of himself in a dream. Also, Sam's absence is accented
from the beginning of the film. At the Department of Records
where Sam works, Mr. Kurtzmann (another of those allegory-like
names), his boss, steps out onto a platform overlooking the workers,
and Kurtzmann calls out, "Has anybody seen Sam Lowry?" No
response. No one, not even the viewer, has seen Sam. Sam is not
noticeable, as is made clear later in a brief chat Sam has with his
friend Jack Lint, as the two pass each other in the huge building that
houses the Department of Records:

> *Jack:* If I'm worried about anyone, Sam, it's you. Sam, whatever hap-
> pened to you? (Jack touches Sam's topcoat).

Jack talks about Sam in the past tense, as if Sam does not exist, or at
least possesses no identity. (Part of his identity is tied into his
clothing, another surface feature, an item which becomes important
later in the film when Sam "rescues" Jill from the state police.) Later
in the conversation, Jack comments on Sam's job at the Department
of Records, saying that it is impossible to get noticed in Sam's
present job. Sam's response is "I know. Wonderful, marvelous,
perfect." The triadic adjective phrase is an echo of the words Jack
has used moments earlier. Apparently, Sam is incapable of formulat-
ing his own phrases, but this does not bother him. He revels in it,
preferring to be transparent. Sam wants to be an absence (like his
father who is absent from the film), so that he can be unreadable.
There is no texture to absence. Despite Jack's encouragement, Sam
refuses to represent himself, relinquishing that responsibility to
whom? An important question here is whether there can be any
such thing as the understanding of that which withholds itself or
remains hidden. Given what Sam says, he does not wish to understand nor to be understood, an act that calls for the presence of
others. Sam wishes to withhold his responsibility for things that go
on around him, as he demonstrates when he tries to defend himself
against Mrs. Terrain, who proposes in an accusatory tone that Sam
do something about the terrorist bombings that have been going on
for thirteen years. Sam's response to Mrs. Terrain is that the bombings are not the responsibility of his department. From Sam's point

of view, he is relieved of his obligations to society by his lack of position. In a society so specialized, so fragmented, Sam's realm of control, of responsibility, is quite small. He cannot even cope with basic malfunctions in his own apartment. More generally, *Brazil* shows us a society without a leader, without someone to take responsibility for a large range of matters. Unlike *1984, Brazil* never shows us Big Brother, only brothers. We see Central Services, but no center. Sam lives in an enucleated society, which might explain why the terrorist bombings prove ineffective. There is no head to kill, and the appendages of the bureaucracy seem to regenerate.

The first time the viewer sees Sam, the viewer does not see Sam. We get caught up in the pool, or whirlpool, of Narcissus, because the viewer's first vision of Sam is Sam's vision of himself. The viewer sees Sam's construction of himself in a dream in which Sam imagines himself to be an Icarus-like hero, a mighty, winged man flying above the clouds. To know the story of Icarus is to know that people who fancy themselves to be Icarus-like are in for a bad fall, or at least a return to Mother Earth. In Sam's case, the fall becomes a return to his mother and things associated with his mother, like the exotic. For example, his mother has a leopard rug in her home, and wears as a hat an upside-down boot covered in leopard skin. (This hat symbolizes the inversion Sam's mother desires; she wants to turn back time, to regain her youth through a face-lift.) The exoticism of Ida Lowry can be tied to the film's title as well, since the country Brazil reminds one of the Amazon and the jungle. As Sam returns to his mother's abode at the end of the film—he goes there with Jill seeking refuge from the police, and he is about to have intercourse with Jill in his mother's bed when the police storm into the room— he also returns to "Brazil," the song, for comfort. In fact, the very words of the 1939 song include the notion of return. In the film, return becomes synonymous with escape. Icarus also ascended to escape a labyrinth, a world that seemed to have no exit.[36] For the moment, the stress of the Icarus image is on the letter 'I,' hence the pronoun, i.e., Sam's narcissistic tendencies, and what becomes of his obsessional desire.

In Sam's dream, a sound, a cry, alters the flight path of Sam/

Icarus, the amalgam of Sam and the Icarus-like hero in his dream. The cry is a woman's voice calling out "Sam!" Sam/Icarus's direction changes with the recognition of his name. By attending to this call, Sam finds a veiled woman who is also hovering about, and Sam/Icarus flies over to her to kiss her through the veil. He kisses the imaginary mouth that utters his name. Another call, this one from Mr. Kurtzmann, reminding Sam that he is absent from work, interrupts his dream. Once again, Sam responds to a call for his presence, his attention.

When we return to Sam's dream, a new figure enters, a large, Samurai-like creature, who—from Sam/Icarus's perspective—has had something to do with the veiled woman being caged. A passage from Theodor Adorno's *Minima Moralia* makes some sense of this great, enigmatic Samurai figure: "Pieces of news, like the repulsive humoristic craze for the Loch Ness Monster and the King Kong film, are collective projections of the monstrous total State. People prepare themselves for its terror by familiarizing themselves with gigantic images."[37] As Sam/Icarus finds out when he removes the Samurai mask, the Samurai is Sam. In an essay, "The Festive Character of Theatre," Gadamer writes: "It is the unsettling gaze of the mask that is pure attention, all surface with nothing behind it, and thus pure expression. It is the rigidity of the puppet on a string that nevertheless dances, the alien shock that shakes our comfortable bourgeois self-confidence and puts at risk the reality in which we feel secure. Here we no longer come to self-knowledge within the sovereign realm of our inwardness. We recognize ourselves as the plaything of mighty, supra-personal forces that condition our being."[38] Sam is behind the image of the total state, for he is a functionary within it, complicit in a bureaucracy, and feeling guilty. Sam knows that a mistake has been made. Archibald Tuttle, heating engineer, was supposed to be taken into custody, but instead people from the Ministry of Information arrested a Mr. Buttle, who died under questioning. Sam visits Buttle's family in "Shangrila Towers" to offer them a check to compensate for their loss, and out of this meeting comes the question, "Where is the body?" Some accounting for the absence of Buttle's body must be made (to establish

Buttle's identity), and the question disturbs Sam, even though Sam himself longs to be absent, to be a missing body, one who will not be noticed or questioned.

Sam's freedom comes from lack of ambition in his job, from his disconnectedness. However, as far as Sam's mother is concerned, his stagnation in his job is a sign of his immaturity. She tells him, "Sam, it's time for you to grow up and accept responsibility. Your poor father would be appalled at your lack of promotion." Growing up means moving vertically, and verticality is what characterizes the total state in *Brazil*. The connection between verticality and power pervades the film. Pauline Kael, in her review of *Brazil,* notes that "the picture has a weirdly ingenious vertical quality: the camera always seems to be moving up and down, rarely across, and this seems like a violation of nature."[39] Most of the buildings in the film look like towers, and, as I have noted, the Buttle family lives in a place called "Shangrila Towers." It is interesting that Jill Layton, whom Sam thinks is a subversive, first appears in the film in a bathtub. Jill is in a horizontal position that conflicts with the dominant vertical. Her resistance to verticality is reflected in her derisive attitude toward anyone or anything connected with the bureaucracy, e.g., she knocks aside a snoopy machine when she goes to the Department of Records to reclaim Mr. Buttle's body.

Mrs. Lowry encourages Sam to move vertically by accepting a promotion Mrs. Lowry has arranged with Deputy Minister Helpmann, who has fond memories of Sam's father. Sam meets the deputy minister at a party Mrs. Lowry throws to celebrate her face lift (another concern with the vertical, i.e., lifting sagging things up). Helpmann calls on Sam for assistance in getting to the bathroom, since he is confined to a wheelchair. Sam lifts Helpmann, makes him vertical so that he might use the urinal. Helpmann's inability to get his own body vertical testifies to his impotence. During the time that Helpmann and Sam are in the bathroom, Helpmann begins to reminisce about Sam's father, who is absent from the film, "a ghost in the machine," says Mr. Helpmann, revealing that he sees the state as a machine and indicating that the presence of Sam's father is still felt despite his absence. In his nostalgia, Helpmann spills some powder on the bathroom sink, and he spells out ERE I AM J H in the powder. ERE I AM J H is an anagram for Jeremiah, the name of Sam's father. The anagram is also a code that operates the elevator that eventually takes Sam to the top of the Ministry of Information. The name Jeremiah can also be linked to the elevator, because Jeremiah is Hebrew for "God will elevate."

Of course, Sam's interest in scaling the vertical, in moving up, is prompted by his desire for Jill Layton, by his desire to keep her horizontal. He wants power over her, as he does in his dream. The desire in his dream and the desire in reality coincide for Sam. To paraphrase Deleuze and Guattari's *Anti-Oedipus,* desire makes its entry when the question "What does it mean?" cannot be answered, or perhaps even asked. In other words, Sam's inability to figure out his own situation, to make sense of the world, leads him to focus his attention on desire. It is important to note that Sam's desire for Jill Layton emerges in a dream. He has an image of a woman in his dream, and this dream-woman appears on a television monitor.[40] Jill then becomes an obsession for Sam, so that a man who was once indifferent to promotion, at times even hostile to it, now craves to move up, to become more involved in MOI, since he believes that a promotion will allow him to gain more information about her. What he craves, however, is information, not understanding, and this leads him to misunderstand the object of his dream. By the end of the film, Sam's desire for Jill Layton leads him to delete her personal records from the central computer. In a sense, then, she exists only for him, as she does in his dream. She is present for him, but absent from society, at least from the state's method of accounting for people.

While Sam's absence is important, he seems at the same time to be omnipresent. Mr. Kurtzmann is looking for Sam at the beginning of the film; Sam's mother worries about him, as does Jack Lint. He is someone who is on many people's minds, or one might say, Sam is "in the air," as he is literally in his dream. As Jill Layton discovers, Sam is not easily gotten rid of. Jill kicks him out of her cab, but Sam comically clings to the cab, popping up all over the outside of the cab as it speeds along. He is an annoyance that people cannot shake off. Even at the end of the film, Sam is nettlesome to his torturers because they "lose" him—Sam escapes into an imaginary world and hums the theme song of *Brazil.* Further torture becomes useless. Although Sam withdraws mentally, his body remains and something must be done with it.

The viewer might read Sam as an embodiment of the film. Sam shows himself to be an empty shell. He might be omnipresent, but his presence makes no difference. In a perverse statement, director Terry Gilliam claims that this "empty shell" of a character who hums the theme song is really a hero. Gilliam says Sam "escapes into madness, which I've always considered a reasonable approach to life in certain situations. To me, that's an optimistic ending. Lowry's imagination is still free and alive; they haven't got that. They may have his body, but they don't have his mind."⁴¹ "Madness is reason" sounds like the slogan "War is Peace" in *1984.* The implications of such postmodernist "logic" need to be questioned, for it is certainly not optimistic that at the end of the film the state bureaucracy triumphs. The mass of people remain subject to a brutal totalitarian state, substantially unaffected by all forms of resistance—even terrorism.

At its most radical, *Brazil* seems to endorse terrorism, one of its major themes. At its most pessimistic, *Brazil* tells its audience that even terrorism is useless against a bureaucratic state (read: United States). In the first five minutes of the film, a bomb explodes in a store displaying eight television sets. One of the TV sets survives the explosion. Terrorism depends on television's survival. The remaining TV set is tuned to an interview program in which Deputy Minister Helpmann is being questioned about terrorism. Although the bombing campaign is in its thirteenth year, the deputy minister is not taking terrorism seriously. The interviewer asks, "What do you believe is behind the increase in terrorist bombing?" Mr. Helpmann replies, "Bad sportsmanship." Obviously, the state does not feel threatened by the bombings.

The relationship between Sam and Jill Layton links up with terrorism as well. Part of Sam's attraction to Jill seems to be his assumption that she is part of a terrorist group. (Again, Sam's attraction to the exotic.) Jill, as Sam's ideal of beauty, is a terrorist. Vicki Hearne is one writer who recognizes the relationship between terror and beauty. Hearne writes, "To know beauty is to know the loss of beauty and thus full angst in the face of the knowledge of death."[42] Sam transfers his own desires for terrorism onto Jill, as the viewer sees when Sam reaches across Jill and floors the accelerator in her truck as they approach a police roadblock. After crashing through the roadblock, Sam is jubilant. Resisting the state brings him joy, though he still does not approve of Jill as a terrorist. He believes a Christmas package she is carrying is a bomb. When Jill proposes that Sam open the package to confirm its innocuous contents, Sam refuses, feigning trust. Throughout the film, there is a repression of terrorism. A bomb goes off while Sam and his mother are having lunch at a restaurant, and no one pays attention to the burned and mutilated bodies, except some of the restaurant workers. A band continues to play in the restaurant, and the waiters put up a partition so that the customers do not make an effort to look. Maurice Blanchot writes about this attitude toward disaster in *L'Ecriture du desastre:* "The disaster ruins everything, all the while leaving everything intact. It does not touch anyone in particular."[43] The repetition of terrorism devalues its impact. In fact, in the world of *Brazil,* terrorism appears to be a "normal" part of life, and no one, other than the person who interviews Mr. Helpmann, attempts to attach motivations or reasons to the terrorism. The traumatic effects of the bombings are absorbed in order to be forgotten. Blanchot says that the disaster is related to forgetfulness. Forgetfulness and withdrawal mark the postmodern scene, at least as it appears in *Brazil.*

III

The victory of the state over the people as portrayed in *Brazil* contradicts the film's references to Sergei Eisenstein's work, particularly *October* and *Battleship Potemkin.* Before addressing the differences between Gilliam's film and Eisenstein's work, I should note the references to Eisenstein's work in *Brazil.* For example, one of Gilliam's quotations of Eisenstein involves a mask work by Jack Lint, a character who tortures people for the state. (*Brazil* tells us that one's worst enemy is one's friend.) The mask, or one very much like it, can be found in the "masks of the gods" montage in *October* (1928). Also, toward the end of *Brazil,* when Sam Lowry imagines he is part of Archibald Tuttle's revolutionary forces, Gilliam presents a repeat of Eisenstein's Odessa steps sequence from *Battleship Potemkin* (1925).[44]

Generally speaking, Eisenstein's films present the viewer with images of mass action. Change comes about through social movement, like the storming of the Winter Palace depicted in *October.* In Eisenstein's films, the state does not crush the people nor force them to retreat into their imaginations, as if imagination were the only place left for freedom. An audience can find hope and commitment in these Eisenstein films, as can be seen from his comments on *Battleship Potemkin:* "I am accused of making *Battleship Potemkin* too emotional. But are we not all people? Don't we have human feelings? Don't we have passions? Don't we have our own tasks and purposes in life? The film was enormously successful in Berlin, and in other parts of post-war Europe that was plunged into the chaos of total instability, and at that time and in those places it sounded a clarion call to a life that was worthy of mankind itself."[45] Here is rhetoric and a concern for bringing some stability to a chaotic situation. Eisenstein tells us that his film serves as a civic argument about what the construction of a life worthy of human beings looks like. By contrast, *Brazil* looks like an example of political despair; one can find little hope for change, either in the diegetic space or in the space of our own society, given that Gilliam meant the film to be a message to the United States. Of course, one could see *Brazil* as a negative example, as a film that might lead viewers to take wary note of the similarities between *Brazil* and contemporary life in the United States. *Brazil* as allegory compels us to see matters in more than one way. One of the few hopes lies in Archibald Tuttle, who is apparently still loose in the world of the film, a kind of Robin Hood or outlaw mechanic. Tuttle understands how things fit together. For example, the labyrinthine structure of ubiquitous pipes and hoses frustrates Sam but not Tuttle. For Sam, the "system," if only of pipes and hoses, is out of control, and his attempts at understanding are repeatedly thwarted.

This sort of frustration also characterizes postmodern politics and art, which is another reason why I think *Brazil* exemplifies postmodernism in its nonarchitectural context. Not to understand is one of postmodernism's goals, and thus postmodernism presents a challenge to understanding. Postmodernists celebrate incoherence, the uninterpretable. In many ways, *Brazil* resists interpretation. In it, one can detect anagrams, allusions to other films, and allegorical elements, but ultimately one is at great pains to piece the puzzle together, partly because the pieces come from many different puzzles. Or, to use another image, the viewer cannot find the key to unlock, say, the end of the film, which takes place in a vast domed structure shaped much like a keyhole, a shape that appears to be an important clue.

Brazil could be seen as an example of an antihermeneutical work, but here I would stress that to call something uninterpretable is still to understand the work in some way. The Heideggerian "as-structure" of understanding is still at work, for the viewer can see *Brazil* as a postmodern film. Something completely alien, completely beyond comprehension would be terrifying. We would be in the realm of the Unspeakable. Further, *Brazil,* like the architectural works Jencks speaks of, displays a surplus of possible meanings. In this sense, it is productive for thinking.

For a more precise notion of postmodernism outside of architecture, we can turn to a proponent of postmodernism, Jean-François Lyotard, who proposes smashing any idea that supports unity of experience. For postmodernists, it is naive to have confidence in the notion of emancipation through social action (Eisenstein). Some postmodernists endorse the death of the social; they prefer neutrality to taking sides in causes, because successful resistance merely substitutes one form of power and oppression for another. Nevertheless, at the end of the essay "What Is Postmodernism?" Lyotard uses militaristic language in his narrative against coherence: "Let us wage war on totality," he writes. "Let us be witnesses to the unpresentable; let us activate the differences and save the honor of the name."[46] As Guattari sees it, "According to Lyotard we must still be extremely suspicious of the least desire for any serious social action. All values that achieve consensus, he says, have become old-fashioned and questionable."[47] Guattari refuses to nod to Lyotard's call to war, as do I.

Brazil reflects postmodernism, for "*Brazil* makes you feel that no rational understanding of the world is possible—that all we have is what T. S. Eliot called 'a heap of broken images.'"[48] In this respect, *Brazil* is a *rocaille* shellwork, made from broken images or shells assembled like a mosaic, a mosaic filled with bits of information. Information plays a key role in postmodernism. At the end of *The Postmodern Condition*, Lyotard urges that data banks be opened to the public in the belief that "language games would then be games of perfect information at any given moment."[49] His suggestion arises, in part, from the postmodern paranoia concerning totalizing effects, and exhausting texts—as if such a thing were possible. Gadamer has shown that understanding is never finished, because, as creatures in history, we are always understanding differently.

Also, Lyotard confuses the relationship between information and understanding. More information in no way necessarily leads to greater understanding. In "What is Practice? The Conditions of Social Reason," Gadamer puts the matter this way: "The increase in the degree of information, then, does not necessarily mean a strengthening of social reason. Instead, it seems to me that the real problem lies right here: the threatening loss of identity by people today. The individual in society who feels dependent and helpless in the face of technically mediated life forms becomes incapable of establishing an identity."[50] Searches for identity and attempts at abolishing identity propel *Brazil*, e.g., the Buttle/Tuttle confusion, and Sam's attempt to "delete" Jill Layton from society. Given the immense bureaucratic structures cemented in place in *Brazil*, people are reduced to functionaries, mere operators of machines. The state and its technology subordinate identity to themselves; human beings can identify themselves only in relation to their positions in institutions or in relation to their attachments to technological devices. It is no coincidence that the acronym for the Ministry of Information is *moi*. A decade before *Brazil,* Gadamer described the situation Terry Gilliam put on film, a world in which, as Gadamer says, "ever fewer people are making the decisions and ever more are manning the apparatus."[51]

Postmodernism continues to search for its identity as well. At present, some postmodernists find the end of this search in what Stanley Rosen calls a "romantic identification with the outcasts and the oppressed."[52] Most postmodernists seem to want nothing to do with identity, as if freedom came from escaping identification, though *Brazil* offers an important lesson about refusing identity: Whether one insists on one's identity, or whether one refuses to be identified—it doesn't matter, because someone will come along and say who you are (the lesson Buttle learns).

> *Sam:* My name is Lowry. Sam Lowry. I have to report to Mr. Warren.
> *Porter:* Thirtieth floor, sir. You're expected.
> *Sam:* Er, don't you want to search me?
> *Porter:* No, sir.
> *Sam:* (taken aback, reaching into his pocket) My ID cards.
> *Porter:* No need, sir.
> *Sam:* But I could be anybody.
> *Porter:* No you couldn't, sir.

Notes

Introduction

1. Hans-Georg Gadamer, "The Hermeneutics of Suspicion," in *Hermeneutics: Questions and Prospects,* ed. Gary Shapiro and Alan Sica (Amherst: University of Massachusetts Press, 1984), p. 55.

2. Paul Zumthor, "From Hi(story) to Poem, or the Paths of Pun: The Grand Rhétoriqueurs of Fifteenth-Century France," *New Literary History* 10 (Winter 1979): 235.

3. Albert Heppner, "The Popular Theatre of the Rederijkers in the Work of Jan Steen and His Contemporaries," *Journal of the Warburg and Courtauld Institutes* 3 (1939/40): 46. Further references will be cited as PTR followed by page number.

4. For some other examples of Steen's work on rhetoricians, see the special issue on Steen in the *Bulletin—Philadelphia Museum of Art* 78 (Winter 1982/Spring 1983). Within that issue is a commentary on *Rhetoricians at a Window,* and much of the information about the painting that appears here is from that commentary (pp. 25–28). Hereafter this will be cited as BP followed by page number. For more on this topic, see François Rigolot, "The *Rhétoriqueurs*" in *A New History of French Literature,* ed. Denis Hollier (Cambridge: Harvard University Press, 1989), 127–33.

5. Gerald L. Bruns, "Tragic Thoughts at the End of Philosophy," *Soundings* 72 (Winter 1989): 711.

6. Brian Vickers, *In Defence of Rhetoric* (Oxford: Clarendon Press, 1988).

7. Hans-Georg Gadamer, "On the Scope and Function of Hermeneutical Reflection," trans. David Linge, in *Philosophical Hermeneutics* (Berkeley: University of California Press, 1976), pp. 18–43.

8. Hans-Georg Gadamer, "*Die Ausdruckskraft der Sprache: Zur Funktion der Rhetorik für die Erkenntnis,*" in *Lob der Theorie* (Frankfurt: Suhrkamp, 1983), pp. 149–63. My colleague Richard Heinemann and I have prepared an English translation of this essay that is in *PMLA* (March 1992). Also see Gadamer's *Rhetorik und Hermeneutik* (Göttingen: Vandenhoeck & Ruprecht, 1976), which includes a discussion of the centrality of rhetoric and hermeneutics not just to the humanities, but to being human (p. 18). My thanks to Dick Schell for making this monograph available to me.

Chapter 1. Simple Hermeneutics of "The Purloined Letter"

1. Terry Eagleton, "Critic as Clown," in *Marxism and the Interpretation of Culture,* ed. Cary Nelson and Lawrence Grossberg (Urbana: University of Illinois Press, 1988), p. 619.

2. For more information about Hermes, see Norman O. Brown's *Hermes the Thief: The Evolution of a Myth* (Madison: University of Wisconsin Press, 1947), and Walter F. Otto's chapter "Hermes" in *The Homeric Gods* (New York: Octagon Books, 1983), pp. 104–24.

3. Gerald L. Bruns, "Structuralism, Deconstruction, and Hermeneutics," *Diacritics* (Spring 1984): 13.

4. Ludwig Wittgenstein, *Remarks on the Philosophy of Psychology,* trans. G.E.M. Anscombe (Chicago: University of Chicago Press, 1980), p. 156.

5. V. N. Volosinov, *Marxism and the Philosophy of Language,* trans. Ladislav Matejka and I. R. Titunik (New York: Seminar Press, 1973), p. 5. I am following the lead of Gary Saul Morson and Caryl Emerson, who in *Mikhail Bakhtin: Creation of a Prosaics* (Stanford: Stanford University Press, 1990) make the case that *Marxism and the Philosophy of Language* is not the work of Bakhtin.

6. Paul Ricoeur, *Hermeneutics and the Human Sciences,* trans. John B. Thompson (Cambridge: Cambridge University Press, 1981), p. 142.

7. Ibid., p. 143.

8. Bruns, "Structuralism," p. 14.

9. This is not to say that history is texts. See "The Politics of Reading Formations: The Case of Nietzsche in Imperial Germany (1870–1919)," in *New German Critique* (Spring/Summer 1983). Also, Gadamer speaks of a broad view of texts in *Philosophical Hermeneutics,* trans. David Linge (Berkeley: University of California Press, 1976): "The hermeneutic aspect itself cannot remain limited to the hermeneutic sciences of art and history, nor to intercourse with 'texts,' and also, not, by extension, to the experience of art itself. The universality of the hermeneutic problem, already recognized by Schleiermacher, has to do with the universe of the reasonable, that is, with anything and everything about which human beings can seek to reach agreement" (p. 180).

10. See Hans-Georg Gadamer's chapter, "Play as the Clue to Ontological Explanation," in *Truth and Method,* trans. Joel Weinsheimer and Donald G. Marshall, 2nd rev. ed. (New York: Crossroad Publishing Co., 1989), pp. 101–34.

11. Gadamer, *Truth and Method,* p. 102.

12. Claude Richard, "Destin, Design, Dasein: Lacan, Derrida, and 'The Purloined Letter,'" *Iowa Review* 12 (Fall 1981): 1.

13. Gadamer, *Truth and Method,* pp. 102–3.

14. Gadamer, *Philosophical Hermeneutics,* p. 24.

15. Ludwig Wittgenstein, *Remarks on the Foundations of Mathematics,* trans. G.E.M. Anscombe (Cambridge: MIT Press, 1978), p. 61.

16. Gadamer, *Truth and Method,* p. 298. All of this is tied to Gadamer's view of the dialogical, which P. Christopher Smith makes clear in his "Plato as Impulse and Obstacle in Gadamer's Development of a Hermeneutical Theory," in *Gadamer and*

Hermeneutics, ed. Hugh Silverman (New York: Routledge, 1991), 23–41. Smith sees that Gadamer is more than a moon to the planet Heidegger, and that Gadamer occasionally eclipses Heidegger.

17. Jacques Lacan, *Ecrits: A Selection,* trans. Alan Sheridan (New York: W. W. Norton, 1977), p. 1.

18. Dominick LaCapra, *History and Criticism* (Ithaca: Cornell University Press, 1985), p. 36.

19. Hans-Georg Gadamer, "Notes on Planning for the Future," *Daedalus* (Spring 1966): 572–89.

20. Gadamer, *Truth and Method,* pp. 124–26.

21. Hans-Georg Gadamer, *Dialogue and Dialectic: Eight Hermeneutical Studies on Plato,* trans. P. Christopher Smith (New Haven: Yale University Press, 1980), pp. 1–20.

22. See Hannelore Rausch, *Theoria: von ihrer sakralen zur philosophischen Bedeutung* (Munich: Wilhelm Fink Verlag, 1982), esp. pp. 18–26. Rausch says, for instance, "*Die Theoroi sind Festgestände, die offiziell von einer Stadt oder Gemeinde nach einer anderen abgeordnet wurden, um dort entweder eine selbständige Kulthandlung vorzunehmen oder an einem Fest jener fremden Gemeinde als Vertreter der Heimatstadt teilzunehmen und . . . Opfer, Tanze, und Spiele durchzuführen*" (pp. 21–22). What I want to emphasize here is the participatory and communal nature of their activities. They are people who take part (*teilnehmen*).

23. Hans-Georg Gadamer, "The Hermeneutics of Suspicion," in *Hermeneutics: Questions and Prospects,* ed. Gary Shapiro and Alan Sica (Amherst: University of Massachusetts Press, 1984), pp. 54–65. Gadamer makes an important point about the connections between rhetoric and hermeneutics in this essay when he makes the distinction between *rhetorica* and *critica:* "*Rhetorica* and *critica* are two competing approaches, insofar as *rhetorica* is obviously based on common sense, on the probability of arguments insofar as they are well received and assured by appearances. On the other hand, the critical attitude stands against appearances, on the side of the new physics, with its insistence on method" (p. 55).

24. Jacques Lacan, "Seminar on the 'The Purloined Letter,'" trans. Jeffrey Mehlman, *Yale French Studies* 48 (1973): 38–76; hereafter cited as SPL followed by page number. Jacques Derrida, "Le facteur de la vérité," in *The Post Card: From Socrates to Freud and Beyond,* trans. Alan Bass (Chicago: University of Chicago Press, 1987), pp. 413–96; hereafter cited as FV followed by page number. Barbara Johnson, "The Frame of Reference: Poe, Lacan, Derrida," *Yale French Studies* 55/56 (1977): 457–505; hereafter cited as FR followed by page number.

25. Gerald L. Bruns, *Inventions: Writing, Textuality, and Understanding in Literary History* (New Haven: Yale University Press, 1982), p. 2.

26. Geoffrey Waite, "The Politics of 'The Question of Style': Nietzsche/ Hö[l]lderlin," in *Identity of the Literary Text,* ed. Mario J. Valdes and Owen Miller (Toronto: University of Toronto Press, 1985), p. 247.

27. Gadamer, *Truth and Method,* p. 309.

28. Ann Jefferson and David Robey, eds., *Modern Literary Theory: A Comparative Introduction* (London: Batsford Academic and Educational, 1982), p. 125. I

agree with Vicki Hearne that "to be 'objective' is to try to approach the condition of being No One in Particular with a view from Nowhere. . . ." See her *Adam's Task: Calling Animals by Name* (New York: Alfred A. Knopf, 1986), p. 229.

29. Geoffrey Hartman, *Saving the Text: Literature/Derrida/Philosophy* (Baltimore: Johns Hopkins University Press, 1981), p. 107.

30. Edgar Allan Poe, *Selected Works* (Middlesex: Penguin Books, 1967), p. 346; hereafter cited as PL followed by page number.

31. Geoffrey Waite, "The Order of Bourgeois Protest," *Studies in Twentieth Century Literature* 10 (Spring 1986): 149–50.

32. Edward Said, "Opponents, Audiences, Constituencies, and Community," in *The Politics of Interpretation,* ed. W.J.T. Mitchell (Chicago: University of Chicago Press, 1983), p. 12.

33. Another reading of this even/odd case appears in Stephen Melville's *Philosophy Beside Itself: On Deconstruction and Modernism* (Minneapolis: University of Minnesota Press, 1986), pp. 88–93. Melville attempts to show that "randomness cannot appear for us except as a random order."

34. Wilhelm Dilthey, *Gesammelte Schriften* VII (Berlin: B. G. Teubner, 1927), p. 136; Wilhelm Dilthey, *Selected Writings,* trans. H. P. Rickman (Cambridge: Cambridge University Press, 1976), p. 181.

35. Gadamer, *Truth and Method,* pp. 302ff.

36. Carlo Ginzburg, "Clues: Morelli, Freud, and Sherlock Holmes," in *The Sign of Three: Dupin, Holmes, Peirce,* ed. Umberto Eco and Thomas A. Sebeok (Bloomington: Indiana University Press, 1976), pp. 81–118.

37. Ernest Mandel, *Delightful Murder: A Social History of the Crime Story* (Minneapolis: University of Minnesota Press, 1984).

38. Ibid., p. 18.

39. Ibid., pp. 16–17, emphasis mine.

40. Stanley Cavell, *In Quest of the Ordinary: Lines of Skepticism and Romanticism* (Chicago: University of Chicago Press, 1988), pp. 153–78.

Chapter 2. Socrates and Cicero, Truth-telling and Lying

1. Gerald L. Bruns, "Response to Hans-Georg Gadamer's 'The Eminent Text and Its Truth,'" *Midwest Modern Language Association Bulletin* (Spring 1980): 14.

2. Hans-Georg Gadamer, *The Relevance of the Beautiful and Other Essays,* ed. Robert Bernasconi, trans. Nicholas Walker (Cambridge: Cambridge University Press, 1986), p. 139. For more on Gadamer's views about poetic speech, see his *Wer bin Ich und wer bist Du? Ein Kommentar zu Paul Celans Gedichtfolge "Atemkristall,"* rev. ed. (Frankfurt: Suhrkamp, 1986)—an English translation by Richard Heinemann and Bruce Krajewski is forthcoming from State University of New York Press.

3. Edmond Jabès, *The Book of Questions,* vol. 1, trans. Rosmarie Waldrop (Middletown, Conn.: Wesleyan University Press, 1976), p. 39.

4. Hans-Georg Gadamer, "*Was Ist Wahrheit?*" *Kleine Schriften I* (Tübingen: J.C.B. Mohr, 1967), pp. 46–58.

5. Robert Nozick, *Philosophical Explanations* (Cambridge: Harvard University Press, 1981), p. 571.

6. Walter Burkert, *Greek Religion,* trans. John Raffan (Cambridge: Harvard University Press, 1985), p. 285.

7. Charles Taylor, "Language and Human Nature," in *Human Agency and Language: Philosophical Papers* 1 (Cambridge: Cambridge University Press, 1985): 215–47; hereafter cited by page number in the text.

8. Cicero, *Murder Trials,* trans. Michael Grant (Middlesex: Penguin Books, 1990), p. 211.

9. Cicero, *Selected Letters,* trans. D. R. Shackleton Bailey (Middlesex: Penguin Books, 1986), p. 73.

10. Cicero does have something to say about constancy, though. See Book I of Cicero's *On Duties* (*De Officiis*), ed. M. T. Griffin and E. M. Atkins (Cambridge: Cambridge University Press, 1991). For those who think the quotations from Cicero make him sound like a scoundrel, see a fine defense of his activities in Christian Habicht's *Cicero the Politician* (Baltimore: Johns Hopkins University Press, 1990).

11. For more about the implications of light and darkness for ancient literary theory, see Wesley Trimpi's "Horace's '*Ut Pictura Poesis*': The Argument for Stylistic Decorum," *Traditio* 34 (1978): esp. 35–49. For a discussion of light in connection to philosophy, see Hans Blumenberg, "*Licht als Metapher der Wahrheit,*" *Studium Generale* 10 (1957): 432–47.

12. P. Harvey, "Aristotle on Truth and Falsity in *De Anima* 3.6," *Journal of the History of Philosophy* 16 (April 1978): 219.

13. Vitruvius, *On Architecture,* trans. Frank Granger (London: Loeb Classical Library, 1931), p. 277.

14. Ibid., p. 279.

15. Hans-Georg Gadamer, *Plato's Dialectical Ethics: Phenomenological Interpretations Relating to the "Philebus,"* trans. Robert M. Wallace (New Haven: Yale University Press, 1991), 98; hereafter cited as PDE followed by page number.

16. Longus, *Daphnis and Chloe,* trans. George Thornley and J. M. Edmonds (London: Loeb Classical Library, 1924), pp. 161–63.

17. E. M. Forster, *A Passage to India* (New York: Harcourt Brace Jovanovich, 1924), p. 149.

18. Ibid., p. 239.

19. Ibid., p. 283.

20. Martin Heidegger, "Plato's Doctrine of Truth," trans. John Barlow, in *Philosophy in the 20th Century,* ed. William Barrett and Henry D. Aiken, vol. 3 (New York: Random House, 1962), p. 260. The importance of caves and cave imagery in both philosophy and literature is the subject of Hans Blumenberg's *Höhlenausgänge* (Frankfurt: Suhrkamp, 1989).

21. Heidegger, "Plato's Doctrine of Truth," p. 261.

22. Piero Pucci, "True and False Discourse in Hesiod," in *Poetry and Poetics from*

Ancient Greece to the Renaissance, ed. G. M. Kirkwood (Ithaca: Cornell University Press, 1975), p. 51.

23. Wesley Trimpi, *Muses of One Mind: The Literary Analysis of Experience and Its Continuity* (Princeton: Princeton University Press, 1983), p. 292.

24. Ben Edwin Perry, *The Ancient Romances* (Berkeley: University of California Press, 1967), p. 76. I came across this source in a dissertation by Ralph Berry, "Telling the Truth: Facts, Lies, and Nonsense in the History of Fiction" (Ph.D. diss., University of Iowa, 1985).

25. Trimpi, *Muses of One Mind,* p. 299.

26. This seemingly outrageous comment appears in Martha C. Nussbaum's *The Fragility of Goodness: Luck and Ethics in Greek Tragedy and Philosophy* (Cambridge: Cambridge University Press, 1986), p. 198. Nussbaum's reading of the *Symposium* reveals that Alcibiades is more human than Socrates, that is, capable of human frailty and flaws, like drunkenness and inappropriateness. While his humanity might keep Alcibiades from the sort of truth Socrates has access to, Socrates' steadfast attitude with regard to truth diminishes his humanity. Socrates appears icy in comparison to Alcibiades.

27. Gerald L. Bruns, *Inventions: Writing, Textuality, and Understanding in Literary History* (New Haven: Yale University Press, 1982), p. 98.

28. J. L. Austin, *Philosophical Papers* (Oxford: Oxford University Press, 1961), p. 132.

29. Stanley Rosen, *Plato's "Sophist": The Drama of Original and Image* (New Haven: Yale University Press, 1983), p. 134.

30. Pucci, "True and False," p. 41.

31. Mario Untersteiner, *The Sophists,* trans. Kathleen Freeman (New York: Philosophical Library, 1954), p. 137.

32. Ibid., pp. 141–42.

33. Hans-Georg Gadamer, "Dialectic and Sophism in Plato's *Seventh Letter,*" in *Dialogue and Dialectic: Eight Hermeneutical Studies on Plato,* trans. P. Christopher Smith (New Haven: Yale University Press, 1980), p. 111. Another valuable work on the sophists and their theory of language is G. B. Kerferd's *The Sophistic Movement* (Cambridge: Cambridge University Press, 1981), esp. pp. 68–77.

34. For more about the thaumaturgical qualities of language, and rhetorical uses of language in particular, see Jacqueline de Romilly, *Magic and Rhetoric in Ancient Greece* (Cambridge: Harvard University Press, 1975).

35. Hans-Georg Gadamer, *Philosophical Hermeneutics,* trans. David Linge (Berkeley: University of California Press, 1976), p. 24.

36. Hans Blumenberg, "An Anthropological Approach to the Contemporary Significance of Rhetoric," in *After Philosophy: End or Transformation?* ed. Kenneth Baynes, James Bohman, and Thomas McCarthy (Cambridge: MIT Press, 1987), pp. 427, 436.

37. Cicero, *Orator* 8. 24 (Loeb trans.).

38. Cicero, *De Oratore* 3. 14 (Loeb trans.).

39. Cicero, *Orator* 28. 99 (Loeb trans.).

40. Cicero, *Orator* 38. 132 (Loeb trans.).

41. Blumenberg, "Anthropological Approach," p. 430.

42. See R.G.A. Buxton, *Persuasion in Greek Tragedy: A Study of "Peitho"* (Cambridge: Cambridge University Press, 1982).

43. Blumenberg, "Anthropological Approach," pp. 437–38.

44. Sissela Bok, *Lying: Moral Choice in Public and Private Life* (New York: Random House, 1978), p. 20. In *Kaironomia: On the Will-to-Invent* (Ithaca: Cornell University Press, 1987), Eric Charles White mentions a statement by Gorgias about tragic drama that casts lies in an unusual light that complements Bok's statement about the power of deception. Gorgias says that tragic drama is "a deception in which the deceiver is more justly esteemed than the nondeceiver and the deceived is wiser than the undeceived." White says, "Tragedy in effect musicalizes dissonance, endowing the contradictory, antithetical character of the truth with a beautiful or comprehensible form" (pp. 39–40). White's first chapter, "The Paradox of the Liar," is a good place to begin studying the ancient Greek perspective on lies and rhetoric.

For more on lies and lying, see Perez Zagorin, *Ways of Lying: Dissimulation, Persecution, and Conformity in Early Modern Europe* (Cambridge: Harvard University Press, 1990), and F. G. Bailey, *The Prevalence of Deceit* (Ithaca: Cornell University Press, 1991). C. Jan Swearingen's *Rhetoric and Irony: Western Literacy and Western Lies* (New York: Oxford University Press, 1991) reached me too late to take it into account.

Chapter 3. Coriolanus

1. Stanley Cavell, "*Coriolanus* and Interpretations of Politics ('Who does the wolf love?')," in *Disowning Knowledge* (Cambridge: Cambridge University Press, 1987), p. 165.

2. Bertolt Brecht, *Collected Plays*, vol. 9, ed. Ralph Mannheim and John Willett (New York: Random House, 1973), p. 393.

3. Hans Blumenberg, "An Anthropological Approach to the Contemporary Significance of Rhetoric," in *After Philosophy: End or Transformation?*, ed. Kenneth Baynes, James Bohman, and Thomas McCarthy (Cambridge: MIT Press, 1987), p. 445.

4. Ibid., p. 437.

5. Hans-Georg Gadamer, *The Relevance of the Beautiful and Other Essays*, ed. Robert Bernasconi, trans. Nicholas Walker (Cambridge: Cambridge University Press, 1986), p. 144.

6. E. C. Pettet, "*Coriolanus* and the Midlands Insurrection of 1607," *Shakespeare Survey* 3 (1950): 35.

7. Cavell, "*Coriolanus*," p. 145.

8. See Felicia Hardison Londre, "Coriolanus and Stavisky: The Interpenetration of Art and Politics," *Theatre Research International* 11 (1986): 119–32.

9. Gerald L. Bruns, *Inventions: Writing, Textuality, and Understanding in Literary History* (New Haven: Yale University Press, 1982), p. 119.

10. Cavell, "*Coriolanus*," p. 163.

11. Gadamer, *Relevance of the Beautiful*, p. 153.

12. Cavell, "*Coriolanus*," p. 146.

13. Brian Vickers, *Shakespeare: Coriolanus* (London: Edward Arnold, 1976), p. 27.

14. Cavell, "*Coriolanus*," p. 149.

15. James Holstun, "Tragic Superfluity in *Coriolanus*," *ELH* 50 (1983): 489.

16. Robert Weimann, "History and the Issue of Authority in Representation: The Elizabethan Theatre and the Reformation," *New Literary History* 17 (Spring 1986): 462.

17. Ibid., p. 473.

18. Gerald L. Bruns, "Cain: Or, the Metaphorical Construction of Cities," *Salmagundi* 74–75 (Spring-Summer 1987): 82.

Chapter 4. Rhetoric in Milton's *Of Education*

1. Hanna H. Gray, "Renaissance Humanism: The Pursuit of Eloquence," *Journal of the History of Ideas* 24 (1963): 501.

2. Annabel Patterson, *Censorship and Interpretation: The Conditions of Writing and Reading in Early Modern England* (Madison: University of Wisconsin Press, 1984), p. 11.

3. Joseph A. Wittreich, Jr., "Milton's Idea of the Orator," *Milton Quarterly* 6 (May 1972): 39.

4. Robert T. Fallon, *Captain or Colonel: The Soldier in Milton's Life and Art* (Columbia: University of Missouri Press, 1984), p. 128.

5. Desiderius Erasmus, *The Education of a Christian Prince*, trans. Lester K. Born (New York: Columbia University Press, 1936), p. 249.

6. John Milton, *Collected Prose Works*, vol. 2, ed. Ernest Sirluck (New Haven: Yale University Press, 1959), p. 354.

7. Samuel Hartlib, *Samuel Hartlib and the Advancement of Learning*, ed. Charles Webster (Cambridge: Cambridge University Press, 1970), p. 4.

8. Ibid., pp. 4–5.

9. Ibid., p. 10.

10. Ruth Mohl, *John Milton and His Commonplace Book* (New York: Frederick Ungar, 1969), p. 125.

11. Milton, *Collected Prose*, pp. 193–94.

12. Hartlib, *Samuel Hartlib*, p. 52.

13. Herman Rapaport, *Milton and the Postmodern* (Lincoln: University of Nebraska Press, 1983), p. 175. Annabel Patterson makes a similar case about Milton's elitism at the end of her "Couples, Canons, and the Uncouth: Spenser-and-Milton in Educational Theory," *Critical Inquiry* 16 (Summer 1990): 792.

14. Rapaport, *Milton*, p. 175.

15. Elizabeth Eisenstein, *The Printing Press as an Agent of Change*, vol. 1 (Cambridge: Cambridge University Press, 1979), p. 63.

16. Milton, *Collected Prose*, pp. 370–71.

17. See Lawrence Stone, "The Educational Revolution in England, 1560–1640," *Past and Present* 28 (1964): 41–80.

18. Ibid., p. 68.

19. Ibid., p. 69.

20. See H. I. Marrou, "Education and Rhetoric," in *The Legacy of Greece: A New Appraisal*, ed. M. I. Finley (Oxford: Oxford University Press, 1981), pp. 185–201.

21. Milton, *Collected Prose*, pp. 378–79.

22. Diane Parkin Speer, " 'Freedom of Speech': Milton's View of Polemic and his Polemical Works," (Ph.D. diss., University of Iowa, 1970), p. 7.

23. Milton, *Collected Prose*, p. 372.

24. Terence Cave, *The Cornucopian Text: Problems of Writing in the French Renaissance* (Oxford: Oxford University Press, 1979), p. 5.

25. Ibid., p. 3.

26. Milton, *Collected Prose*, pp. 411–12.

27. Nicolo Machiavelli, *The Chief Works and Others,* trans. Allan Gilbert (Durham: Duke University Press, 1965), p. 661.

28. Ibid., p. 661.

29. Ibid., p. 587.

30. Dominic A. LaRusso, "Rhetoric and Diplomatic Training in Venice, 1450–1590," *Western Speech* (Spring 1959): 70.

31. Nancy S. Struever, *The Language of History in the Renaissance: Rhetoric and Historical Consciousness in Florentine Humanism* (Princeton: Princeton University Press, 1970), p. 102. Also see her chapter, "Rhetoric and Politics," pp. 101–15.

32. Brian Vickers, " 'The Power of Persuasion': Images of the Orator, Elyot to Shakespeare," in *Renaissance Eloquence: Studies in the Theory and Practice of Renaissance Rhetoric,* ed. James J. Murphy (Berkeley: University of California Press, 1983), p. 415.

33. Quoted in William Riley Parker, *Milton* (Oxford: Oxford University Press, 1968), p. 246.

34. John M. Steadman, "Milton's Rhetoric: Satan and the 'Unjust Discourse,' " in *Milton Studies,* vol. 1, ed. James D. Simmonds (Pittsburgh: University of Pittsburgh Press, 1969), p. 89.

35. John Milton, *Complete Poems and Major Prose,* ed. Merritt Hughes (New York: Odyssey Press, 1957), p. 605.

36. See Irene Samuel, "Milton and the Province of Rhetoric," *Milton Studies,* vol. 10 (Pittsburgh: University of Pittsburgh Press, 1977), p. 177.

37. Milton, *Complete Poems,* p. 728.

38. Parker, *Milton,* pp. 222–23.

39. Speer, "Freedom of Speech," p. 16.

40. Aristotle, *Rhetoric,* trans. John Freese (Cambridge: Harvard University Press, 1926), p. 457.

41. Milton, *Complete Poems,* p. 624.

42. Thomas O. Sloane, in his *Donne, Milton, and the End of Humanist Rhetoric* (Berkeley: University of California Press, 1985), seeks to make Milton out to be a Ramist, mostly on the basis that Milton wrote a Ramist text on logic. Sloane also

seems to reduce "good" rhetoric in the Renaissance to rhetoric that dealt with *controversia* (see Sloane, p. 219).

43. Walter J. Ong, *Ramus: Method and the Decay of Dialogue* (Cambridge: Harvard University Press, 1958), p. 41.

44. Milton, *Collected Prose,* pp. 402–3.

45. See Brian Vickers, "Epideictic and Epic in the Renaissance," *New Literary History* 14 (Spring 1983): 507.

46. Patterson, *Censorship,* p. 46. Patterson teaches her audience to read Renaissance texts differently, i.e., differently in view of censorship. She writes, "Censorship encouraged the use of historical or other uninvented texts such as translations from the classics, which both allowed an author to limit his authorial responsibility for the text . . . and, paradoxically, provided an interpretive mechanism" (p. 57). In addition, according to Patterson, we need to pay more attention to the beginnings of these texts. "Late modern criticism has not paid enough attention to the interpretive status of introductory materials in early modern texts. All too often given over to the province of bibliographers, or even omitted from standard editions, dedications, engraved title pages, commendatory poems and epigraphs are lost to sight. Yet often their function is to alert the reader to his [sic] special responsibilities" (p. 48).

For the continuation of censorship in the Restoration, see Steven N. Zwicker, "Politics and Literary Practice in the Restoration," in *Renaissance Genres: Essays on Theory, History, and Interpretation,* ed. Barbara K. Lewalski (Cambridge: Harvard University Press, 1986), pp. 268–98. For more on this matter before the Restoration, see Lois Potter, *Secret Rites and Secret Writing: Royalist Literature, 1641–1660* (Cambridge: Cambridge University Press, 1989).

47. John Southerden Burn, *The Star Chamber: Notices of the Court and Its Proceedings* (London 1870), p. 129, as cited in Patterson.

Chapter 5. Andgame

1. Maurice Blanchot, "Everyday Speech," *Yale French Studies* 73 (1987): 14.

2. Samuel Beckett, *Endgame* (New York: Grove Press, 1958), p. 58. I have learned much about the play from Stanley Cavell's fine essay, "Ending the Waiting Game: A Reading of Beckett's *Endgame*," in *Must We Mean What We Say?* (New York: Cambridge University Press, 1969), pp. 115–62.

3. See Fania Pascal's account of Wittgenstein's life in *Wittgenstein: Sources and Perspectives,* ed. C. G. Luckhardt (Ithaca: Cornell University Press, 1979), p. 25. Also see Terry Eagleton's "Wittgenstein's Friends," *New Left Review* (Sept./Oct. 1982): 64–90.

4. Richard Rorty, *Consequences of Pragmatism* (Minneapolis: University of Minnesota Press, 1982), p. 19.

5. Ludwig Wittgenstein, *Tractatus Logico-Philosophicus,* trans. D. F. Pears and B. F. McGuinness (London: Routledge and Kegan Paul, 1961), p. 3.

6. Ibid., p. 4.

7. Beckett, *Endgame,* p. 57.

8. See Ian Hacking, *Why Does Language Matter to Philosophy?* (Cambridge: Cambridge University Press, 1975).

9. W.V.O. Quine, *Theories and Things* (Cambridge: Harvard University Press, 1981), p. 189.

10. Ludwig Wittgenstein, *Remarks on the Foundations of Mathematics,* trans. G.E.M. Anscombe (Cambridge: MIT Press, 1978), p. 52.

11. Ibid., p. 165.

12. Ibid., pp. 61, 81.

13. David Bloor, *Wittgenstein: A Social Theory of Knowledge* (New York: Columbia University Press, 1983), pp. 2–3.

14. Henry Staten, *Wittgenstein and Derrida* (Lincoln: University of Nebraska Press, 1984), pp. 75, 66.

15. Ludwig Wittgenstein, *The Blue and Brown Books* (New York: Harper and Row, 1958), p. 25.

16. Mikhail Bakhtin, *The Dialogic Imagination,* trans. Caryl Emerson and Michael Holquist (Austin: University of Texas Press, 1981), p. 293.

17. Ludwig Wittgenstein, *On Certainty,* ed. G.E.M. Anscombe and G. von Wright, trans. Denis Paul and G.E.M. Anscombe (New York: Harper and Row, 1969), p. 32.

18. Katerina Clark and Michael Holquist, *Mikhail Bakhtin* (Cambridge: Harvard University Press, 1984), p. 179. See also Gary Saul Morson's "Bakhtin and the Present Moment," *The American Scholar* (Spring 1991): 201–22.

19. Tzvetan Todorov, *Mikhail Bakhtin: The Dialogical Principle,* trans. Wlad Godzich (Minneapolis: University of Minnesota Press, 1984), p. 33.

20. Ibid., p. 95.

21. Ibid., p. 96.

22. Mikhail Bakhtin, *Problems of Dostoevsky's Poetics,* ed. and trans. Caryl Emerson (Minneapolis: University of Minnesota Press, 1984), p. 287.

23. Gerald L. Bruns, *Inventions: Writing, Textuality, and Understanding in Literary History* (New Haven: Yale University Press, 1982), p. 123.

24. Ludwig Wittgenstein, *Remarks on the Philosophy of Psychology,* vols. 1 and 2, vol. 1 trans. G.E.M. Anscombe, vol. 2 trans. C. G. Luckhardt and M.A.E. Aue (Chicago: University of Chicago Press, 1980), p. 108; hereafter, references to both volumes will be cited in text with volume number followed by entry number.

25. Mikhail Bakhtin, *Art and Answerability: Early Philosophical Essays by M. M. Bakhtin,* ed. Michael Holquist and Vadim Liapunov (Austin: University of Texas Press, 1990), p. 1.

26. Gary Saul Morson and Caryl Emerson, *Mikhail Bakhtin: Creation of a Prosaics* (Stanford: Stanford University Press, 1990), p. 23.

27. Stanley Cavell, *This New Yet Unapproachable America* (Albuquerque: Living Batch Press, 1989), p. 66; hereafter cited as UA, followed by page number.

28. Wittgenstein, *Remarks on Mathematics,* p. 205.

29. Hans Blumenberg, *Höhlenausgänge* (Frankfurt: Suhrkamp, 1989). "*Im Fliegenglas,*" the chapter on Wittgenstein, is on pp. 751–92.

30. Francis Goodrich, Albert Hackett, and Frank Capra, *It's a Wonderful Life,* Screenplay (New York: St. Martin's Press, 1986), p. 210.

Chapter 6. A Reading of Derrida's "White Mythology"

1. Hans-Georg Gadamer, "Heidegger's Paths," *Philosophic Exchange* 2 (Summer 1979): 91.

2. Hans Blumenberg, *Work on Myth,* trans. Robert M. Wallace (Cambridge: MIT Press, 1985), p. 288.

3. Allan Megill, *Prophets of Extremity: Nietzsche, Heidegger, Foucault, Derrida* (Berkeley: University of California Press, 1985), p. 254.

4. References below will give page numbers to both the English and French texts: Jacques Derrida, "White Mythology: Metaphor in the Text of Philosophy," in *Margins of Philosophy,* trans. Alan Bass (Chicago: University of Chicago Press, 1982), pp. 209–71; and "*La mythologie blanche (la metaphore dans le texte philosophique),*" *Poetique* 5 (1971): 1–52.

5. See Hans-Georg Gadamer's "Letter to Dallmayr," trans. Richard Palmer and Diane Michelfelder, in *Dialogue and Deconstruction: The Gadamer-Derrida Encounter* (Albany: State University of New York Press, 1989), pp. 93–101; hereafter cited by page number. A fine account of Gadamer's view of metaphor can be found in Joel Weinsheimer, *Philosophical Hermeneutics and Literary Theory* (New Haven: Yale University Press, 1991), 64–86.

6. Jacques Derrida, "The *Retrait* of Metaphor," *Enclitic* 2 (Fall 1978): 6.

7. Jacques Derrida, *Positions,* trans. Alan Bass (Chicago: University of Chicago Press, 1981), p. 14.

8. Ibid., p. 53.

9. Blumenberg, "*Licht als Metapher der Wahrheit,*" *Studium Generale* 10 (1957): 432. All translations from this text are my own.

10. Ibid., p. 433.

11. Rodolphe Gasché, *The Tain of the Mirror: Derrida and the Philosophy of Reflection* (Cambridge: Harvard University Press, 1986), p. 308.

12. Blumenberg, *Work on Myth,* p. 238. All further references to this text will be cited by page number within the text. In a strikingly similar discussion about worn-out language, Blumenberg addresses an argument put forth by E. Rothacker in his *Philosophische Anthropologie.* Rothacker's discourse is not very different from Derrida's in "White Mythology." This is the passage from *Work on Myth:*

> Pregnance is resistance to factors that efface, that promote diffusion; resistance especially to time, which nevertheless is suspected of being able to produce pregnance through the process of aging. This suggests a contradiction, or at least a difficulty.
>
> I want to illustrate the difficulty by means of the comparison with which Rothacker tries to make plausible the relationship between pregnance and time: "The imprinted forms have a quite singular durability, inflexibility. The imprint is not easy to obliterate. Once the imprinted forms are there, they are difficult to alter. . . . Their being imprinted and even the tangibility that is added to that

have a conserving effect. Thanks to this they stand firm in the temporal flux, just as stones simply outlast the passage of time. Stones over which the mountain torrent flows stand still, they are there. The water flows, the stone stands still. It is true that stones can be worn away by water, but that takes quite a long time; they may also be carried further along, they may also be hit by rocks that are rolling with them and be damaged, but they have durability in time." To be sure, Rothacker immediately reduces his claim, saying that the image of the stone and the mountain torrent exaggerates the duration of the imprinted forms somewhat: They are not as firm as stones, only much firmer than sand castles that summer vacationers make on the ocean beach.

But the image is not only too strong, it is positively wrong. Time does not wear away instances of pregnance; it brings things out in them . . . (p. 69).

13. Lawrence Weschler, "Onward and Upward with the Arts (Boggs—Part 1)," *New Yorker* (January 18, 1988): 33.

14. Ibid., pp. 43–44.

15. Geoffrey Hartman, *Saving the Text: Philosophy/Derrida/Literature* (Baltimore: Johns Hopkins University Press, 1981), p. 137.

16. Weschler, "Onward and Upward," p. 41.

17. Paul Ricoeur, *The Rule of Metaphor: Multidisciplinary Studies of the Creation of Meaning in Language,* trans. Robert Czerny, Kathleen McLaughlin, and John Costello (Toronto: University of Toronto Press, 1977), p. 290.

18. Blumenberg, *"Paradigmen zu einer Metaphorologie," Archiv für Begriffsgeschichte* 6 (1960): 11. My translation.

19. Friedrich Nietzsche, "On Truth and Lies in a Nonmoral Sense," in *Philosophy and Truth: Selections from Nietzsche's Notebooks of the Early 1870's,* trans. and ed. Daniel Breazeale (Atlantic Highlands, N.J.: Humanities Press, 1979), p. 82.

20. For other similarities, see Gustave Gerber's *Die Sprache als Kunst,* 2 vols. (Berlin: R. Gaertners Verlag, 1st. ed., 1871).

21. J. Hillis Miller, "Dismembering and Disremembering in Nietzsche's 'On Truth and Lies in a Nonmoral Sense,'" in *Why Nietzsche Now?* ed. Daniel O'Hara (Bloomington: Indiana University Press, 1985), p. 50.

22. Geoff Waite, "The Politics of 'The Question of Style': Nietzsche/Hö[l]derlin, in *Identity of the Literary Text,* ed. Mario J. Valdes and Owen Miller (Toronto: University of Toronto Press, 1985).

23. Tennessee Williams, *A Streetcar Named Desire* (New York: New American Library, 1947), p. 15.

24. Ibid., p. 88.

25. Ibid., p. 116.

26. Emmanuel Levinas, *Nine Talmudic Readings,* trans. Annette Aronowicz (Bloomington: Indiana University Press, 1990), p. 34.

Chapter 7. Against Clarity

1. Frank Kermode, *The Genesis of Secrecy: On the Interpretation of Narrative* (Cambridge: Harvard University Press, 1979), p. 14.

2. Hannah Arendt, *Between Past and Future: Eight Exercises in Political Thought* (Middlesex: Penguin Books, 1968), p. 186.

3. Martha Nussbaum, *The Fragility of Goodness: Luck and Ethics in Greek Tragedy and Philosophy* (Cambridge: Cambridge University Press, 1986), p. 225.

4. Joseph Leo Koerner, *Die Suche nach dem Labyrinth: Der Mythos von Daedalus und Ikarus* (Frankfurt: Suhrkamp, 1983). All translations from this text are my own.

5. Ibid., p. 36.

6. Ruskin is quoted in J. Hillis Miller's "Ariadne's Thread: Repetition and the Narrative Line," *Critical Inquiry* 3 (1976): 59.

7. See William F. Jackson Knight, *Cumaean Gates: A Reference to the Sixth Aeneid to the Initiation Patter* (Oxford: Basil Blackwell, 1936), especially the chapter "Knossos," pp. 132–48, which discusses the labyrinth's association with caves and with the maze dance "said to have been instituted by Theseus at Delos to commemorate his rescue by Ariadne" (p. 137). For more on labyrinths, see Penelope Reed Doob, *The Idea of the Labyrinth: From Classical Antiquity through the Middle Ages* (Ithaca: Cornell University Press, 1990).

8. Arendt, *Between Past and Future,* p. 188.

9. Ibid., p. 189.

10. See Knight, *Cumaen Gates,* pp. 50–57.

11. Arendt, *Between Past and Future,* p. 183.

12. See P. J. Enk, *"De Labyrinthi Imagine in Foribus Templi Cumani Inscripta,"* *Mnemosyne,* Series 4, 11 (1958): 322–30.

13. Koerner, *Die Suche,* p. 36.

14. Michel Foucault gives another reading of the Minotaur. He says, "At the center of the labyrinth lies the birth. . . ." See his *Death and the Labyrinth: The World of Raymond Roussel,* trans. Charles Ruas (New York: Doubleday and Co., 1986), p. 88.

15. Ibid., pp. 93–94.

16. Jorge Luis Borges, *Labyrinths: Selected Stories and Other Writings,* ed. Donald A. Yates and James E. Irby (New York: New Directions, 1964), pp. 76–87. Of course, the image of the labyrinth appears frequently in Borges's work. Another story that relates to matters discussed here is "Ibn Hakkan al-Bokhari, Dead in His Labyrinth," in *The Aleph and Other Stories 1933–1969,* trans. Norman Thomas Di Giovanni (New York: E. P. Dutton, 1970), pp. 115–25. For the connection between Borges and Poe, see John T. Irwin, "A Clew to a Clue: Locked Rooms and Labyrinths in Poe and Borges," *Raritan* (Spring 1991): 40–57.

17. Borges, *Labyrinths,* p. 85.

18. Ibid., p. 87.

19. Hans-Georg Gadamer, *"Unterwegs zur Schrift?",* in *Schrift und Gedächtnis: Beiträge zur Archaeologies der literarischen Kommunikation,* ed. Aleida and Jan Assmann and Christof Hardmeier (Munich: Wilhelm Fink Verlag, 1983), pp. 10–19.

20. Ibid., p. 12.

21. Ibid., p. 11.

22. Ibid., p. 13. Elsewhere Gadamer says, "Self-understanding is in all its forms

the extremest opposite of self-consciousness and self-possession. Rather, it is an understanding that always places itself in question. . . ." This quotation comes from a letter to Fred Dallmayr about Dallmayr's essay "On Hermeneutics and Deconstruction: Gadamer and Derrida in Dialogue." See Diane P. Michelfelder and Richard E. Palmer, ed., *Dialogue and Deconstruction: The Gadamer-Derrida Encounter* (Albany: State University of New York Press, 1989), p. 95.

23. Martha Nussbaum, " 'This story isn't true': Madness, Reason, and Recantation in the *Phaedrus*," pp. 200–233.

24. Ibid., p. 209.

25. Ibid., p. 225.

26. Ibid., p. 232. For a more detailed account linking eroticism and writing, see Anne Carson, *Eros the Bittersweet: An Essay* (Princeton: Princeton University Press, 1986).

27. Richard Lanham, *Literacy and the Survival of Humanism* (New Haven: Yale University Press, 1983), p. 10. Of course, Strunk and White's *Elements of Style* is still used in many writing programs. However, the following excerpts are from other textbooks currently in use in writing programs around the country, and many of them refer not to writing, but to the "writing process," an indication of how corrupt matters have become. "Our textbook is based on the assumption that you will write more effectively if you clarify your purpose in writing. . . . In the latter chapters of the book, the tasks become more analytic, and you will be asked, for example, to explain why an idea that you hold is sensible or to argue why a position that you take is valid" (p. xi). "The final version of your essay, however, should be clearly guided by one well-defined idea" (p. 102). "In critical thinking . . . the appeal to the reader's intelligence should be paramount and figurative language used with great care so that you do not appear to undermine your objectivity" (p. 421). These quotations are from Linda C. Stanley, David Shimkin, and Allen H. Lanner, *Ways to Writing: Purpose, Task, and Process,* 2d ed. (New York: Macmillan, 1988). In a preface in another textbook, we find, "One focus of this text, then, will be for you to consider and enlarge your writing process, to get beyond the confusion and scary mystery and learn the methods that have worked for other writers" (p. xi). "You should try to get away from your paper between steps, even if you just put it aside for a little while, so that you can return to it as an objective editor" (p. 265). These quotations are from Katherine H. Adams and John L. Adams, *The Accomplished Writer: Observing, Judging, Reflecting* (Englewood Cliffs, N.J.: Prentice Hall, 1988). Another book about the "writing process," in its ninth edition, has a section on "Revising for Clarity": "This section is concerned only with revising confusing sentence structure, even though lack of clarity can result from faulty grammar or punctuation, misleading pronoun reference, or vague or ambiguous wording, as well. Unclear sentence structure sometimes occurs when a writer tries to pack too much information into one sentence" (p. 197). The example used to illustrate this point is a sentence of 108 words. "This involved structure is hard going for both writer and reader. The goal of revision should be to simplify the structure by reducing the number of clauses." These quotations come from Joseph F. Trimmer and James M. McCrimmon, *Writing with a Purpose* (Boston: Houghton Mifflin,

1988). I would like to thank Hilary Siebert for allowing me to borrow these wretched textbooks.

28. J. L. Austin, *Philosophical Papers* (Oxford: Oxford University Press, 1961), p. 132.

29. Ibid., p. 133.

30. Emmanuel Levinas, *Nine Talmudic Readings,* trans. Annette Aronowicz (Bloomington: Indiana University Press, 1990), p. 64. Enigmatic texts were not "problematic" for the ancients. See Gerald L. Bruns, "The Problem of Figuration in Antiquity," in *Hermeneutics: Questions and Prospects,* ed. Gary Shapiro and Alan Sica (Amherst: University of Massachusetts Press, 1984), pp. 147–64. Bruns says, "The ancients would say simply that figuration enables us to understand what is written" (p. 163). Also, the ancients knew something about untrue writing. In the story of Theseus, Theseus leaves Ariadne after escaping from the labyrinth, even though he is supposed to return to her. While Ariadne waits on Naxos for Theseus, the women of Naxos write letters that they give to Ariadne. They tell her that the letters are from Theseus, so that Ariadne will think he has not abandoned her.

31. Arendt, *Between Past and Future,* pp. 171 and 181. Gadamer writes, "Admittedly, it is primarily persons that have authority; but the authority of persons is ultimately based, not on the subjection and abdication of reason but on an act of acknowledgment and knowledge—the knowledge, namely, that the other is superior to oneself in judgment and insight and that for this reason his judgment takes precedence. . . ." See *Truth and Method,* 2nd rev. ed., trans. Joel Weinsheimer and Donald G. Marshall (New York: Crossroad Publishing, 1989), p. 279.

32. Niccolo Machiavelli, *The Discourses of Niccolo Machiavelli* (New Haven: Yale University Press, 1950), p. 479.

33. Carlo Ginzburg, *The Cheese and the Worms: The Cosmos of a Sixteenth-Century Miller,* trans. John Tedeschi and Anne Tedeschi (Baltimore: Johns Hopkins University Press, 1980), pp. 2, 37, 9, 49.

34. A humorous scene in *Brazil* parodies this inquisitorial practice.

35. See Paul Ricoeur, *Interpretation Theory: Discourse and the Surplus of Meaning* (Fort Worth: Texas Christian University Press, 1976), and his essay "Metaphor and the Central Problem of Hermeneutics," in *Hermeneutics and the Human Sciences,* trans. John B. Thompson (Cambridge: Cambridge University Press, 1981), pp. 165–81.

36. Giambattista Vico, *Selected Writings,* trans. Leon Pompa (Cambridge: Cambridge University Press, 1982), p. 42.

37. Stanley Morison, *Politics and Script: Aspects of Authority and Freedom in the Development of Graeco-Latin Script from the Sixth Century B.C. to the Twentieth Century A.D.* (Oxford: Oxford University Press, 1972), p. 31.

38. Ibid., p. 58.

39. Another famous strange text is the so-called Voynich manuscript. See John Manly, "Roger Bacon and the Voynich Ms," *Speculum* 6 (1931): 345–91. I learned of Maimonides' text in Bruns's *Inventions.*

40. Leo Strauss, "Persecution and the Art of Writing," in *Persecution and the Art of Writing* (Glencoe, Ill.: The Free Press, 1952), p. 25. Also see James C. Scott,

Domination and the Arts of Resistance: Hidden Transcripts (New Haven: Yale University Press, 1990), especially the chapter "Voice under Domination: The Arts of Political Disguise," pp. 136–82.

41. See "The Red Wizard of Oz," in *New Masses* (October 4, 1938). See also Jack Zipes, *Fairy Tales and the Art of Subversion* (New York: Wildman Press, 1983), pp. 122–23.

42. *Skiagraphia* is normally translated as "shadow painting." See the entry in *Paulys Real-Encyclopädie der Klassischen Altertumswissenschaft* (Stuttgart: J. B. Metzlersche Verlag, 1931), pp. 979–81. Since no one seems to know what *skiagraphia* means, I have decided to alter its meaning for my own purposes. Also see Wesley Trimpi, "The Early Metaphorical Uses of *skiagraphia* and *skenographia*," *Traditio* 34 (1978): 403–13. My thanks to Laura McClure for her help with questions about the Greek.

43. Hans-Georg Gadamer, *Dialogue and Dialectic: Eight Hermeneutical Studies on Plato* (New Haven: Yale University Press, 1980), p. 111.

44. V. I. Lenin, *Collected Works*, vol. 32 (Moscow: Progress Publishers, 1973), pp. 92–95. The text goes like this:

> When Comrade Bukharin speaks of "logical" grounds, his whole reasoning shows that he takes—unconsciously, perhaps—the standpoint of formal or scholastic logic, and not of dialectical or Marxist logic. Let me explain this by taking the simple example which Comrade Bukharin himself gives. In the December 30 discussion he said: "Comrades, many of you may find that the current controversy suggests something like this: two men come in and invite each other to define the tumbler on the lectern. One says: 'It is a glass cylinder, and a curse on anyone who says different.' The other one says: 'A tumbler is a drinking vessel, and a curse on anyone who says different.' " The reader will see that Bukharin's example was meant to give me a popular explanation of the harm of one-track thinking. I accept it with gratitude, and in the one-good-turn-deserves-another spirit offer a popular explanation of the difference between dialectics and eclecticism.
>
> A tumbler is assuredly both a glass cylinder and a drinking vessel. But there are more than these two properties, qualities, or facets to it; there are an infinite number of them, an infinite number of "mediacies" and inter-relationships with the rest of the world. A tumbler is a heavy object which can be used as a missile; it can serve as a paperweight, a receptacle for a captive butterfly, or a valuable object with an artistic engraving or design, and this has nothing at all to do with whether or not it can be used for drinking, is made of glass, is cylindrical or not quite, and so on and so forth. Moreover, if I needed a tumbler just now for drinking, it would not in the least matter how cylindrical it was, and whether it was actually made of glass; what would matter though would be whether it had any holes in the bottom, or anything that would cut my lips when I drank, etc. But if I did not need a tumbler for drinking but for a purpose that could be served by any glass cylinder, a tumbler with a cracked bottom or without one at all would do just as well, etc.

For those who find an example by Lenin troublesome, here is one by G. K. Chesterton, which demonstrates that Chesterton's Father Brown exemplifies some-one who is skilled at *dissoi logoi*. Could we teach students to be as dextrous as Father

Brown, who in "The Honour of Israel Gow" shows off his rhetorical cunning? In this story, Father Brown travels to Scotland to investigate the life and death of the Earl of Glengyle. For those with Father Brown, the consensus is that Lord Glengyle was a maniac. Inspector Craven from Scotland Yard, in a search of Glengyle Castle, finds a strange inventory of items, four in particular: snuff, diamonds, wax, loose clockwork. Then Craven issues what Father Brown takes as a challenge. Craven says, "The core of the tale we could imagine [i.e., Lord Glengyle's death]; it is the fringes that are mysterious. By no stretch of fancy can the human mind connect together snuff and diamonds and wax and loose clockwork." Father Brown proceeds to give three plausible accounts that nicely connect the four items, and each time Father Brown's audience asks him whether he thinks he has given the true explanation. "I don't think it the true explanation," replied the priest placidly; "but you said that nobody could connect the four things." From G. K. Chesterton, *The Innocence of Father Brown* (Middlesex: Penguin Books, 1983), pp. 117–18.

45. Milton Glaser, "I Listen to the Market," in *On Signs,* ed. Marshall Blonsky (Baltimore: Johns Hopkins University Press, 1985), pp. 467–74.

46. Quoted in "Surveillance," *Mother Jones,* December 1984, pp. 27 and 51.

47. Ralph E. Weber, *United States Diplomatic Codes and Ciphers, 1775–1938* (Chicago: Precedent Publishing, 1979). See also Edgar Allan Poe, "A Few Words on Secret Writing," in *Essays and Reviews* (New York: Library of America, 1984), pp. 1277–91; and James Westfall Thompson and Saul Padover, *Secret Diplomacy: Espionage and Cryptography 1500–1815* (New York: Frederick Ungar Co., 1963). There is an excellent article on Elizabeth and William Friedman, perhaps the best U.S. cryptologists in this century. See James R. Chiles, "Breaking Codes Was This Couple's Lifetime Career," *Smithsonian* (June 1987): 128–44. This article begins with a strange photograph of Friedman's cryptology class posed in such a way that the body positions spell out "Knowledge is power."

48. Arendt, *Between Past and Future,* p. 190.

49. Ibid., p. 196. For another perspective on this same issue, see Richard Sennett's *Authority* (New York: Alfred A. Knopf, 1980), especially the chapter "Autonomy, an Authority without Love," in which Sennett says, "The dominant forms of authority in our lives are destructive; they lack nurturance—the love which sustains others—is a basic human need, as basic as eating or sex. Compassion, trust, reassurance are qualities it would be absurd to associate with these figures of authority in the adult world" (p. 120).

50. Quoted in Miller, "Ariadne's Thread," p. 59. In one version of the myth, it is Daedalus who gives the thread to Ariadne to give to Theseus.

Chapter 8. Postmodernism, Allegory, and Hermeneutics in *Brazil*

1. Hans-Georg Gadamer, *The Relevance of the Beautiful and Other Essays,* ed. Robert Bernasconi, trans. Nicholas Walker (Cambridge: Cambridge University Press, 1986), p. 29.

2. Ibid., p. 10.

3. Gerald L. Bruns, "What Is Tradition?" *New Literary History* 22 (Winter 1991): 17.

4. Gadamer, *Relevance,* p. 49.

5. Ibid., p. 48.

6. Stanley Rosen, *Hermeneutics as Politics* (New York: Oxford University Press, 1987), p. 27.

7. Marxist critics in particular have been worried about postmodernism. In "Postmodernism and Consumer Culture," for instance, Fredric Jameson accuses postmodernists of reinforcing the logic of consumer capitalism, and discusses postmodernism in relation to schizophrenia. See Jameson's article in *The Anti-Aesthetic: Essays on Postmodern Culture,* ed. Hal Foster (Port Townsend, Wash.: Bay Press, 1983), pp. 111–25. According to Foster, the absence of History constitutes the postmodern void. He writes, "Does not the relativism of pastiche (its implosion of period signs) erode the very ability to place historical references—to think historically at all? To put it simply, the Postmodern Style of History may in fact signal the disintegration of style and the collapse of history." See Foster's *Recodings: Art, Spectacle, Cultural Politics* (Port Townsend, N.Y.: Bay Press, 1985).

In language equally as strong as Foster's, Richard Wolin calls postmodernism a "diabolical turn of events," and sees it as a "brave new world of systems theory cybernetics." See his "Modernism and Postmodernism" in *Telos* (Winter 1984–85): 9–29. Italian art historian Giulio Carlo Argan also objects to postmodernism as a kind of "antihistory," since postmodernism indicates "the abandonment of any goal, or design, the lack of all ideological pressure and of any new quest for values." See Argan's "History and Antihistory" in *Flash Art* 125 (December 1985/January 1986): 54–55.

New German Critique devoted its Fall 1984 issue to the topic "Modernity and Postmodernity." The articles dealing with postmodernism's lack of foundation and lack of purpose include: Fredric Jameson's "The Politics of Theory: Ideological Positions in the Postmodernism Debate," pp. 53–66; Seyla Benhabib, "Epistemologies of Postmodernism: A Rejoinder to Jean-François Lyotard," pp. 103–26; and Gerald Raulet, "From Modernity as One-Way Street to Postmodernity as Dead End," pp. 155–77.

8. Ihab Hassan, *The Postmodern Turn: Essays in Postmodern Theory and Culture* (Columbus: Ohio State University Press, 1987), p. 85.

9. Robert Venturi, *Complexity and Contradiction in Architecture* (New York: Museum of Modern Art, 1966), p. 16.

10. Ibid.

11. Charles Jencks, *Architecture Today* (New York: Abrams, 1982), p. 111. For more on the allegorical side of this architecture, see Jencks's *Post-Modernism: The New Classicism in Art and Architecture* (New York: Rizzoli, 1987), pp. 101–24; and David Kolb's *Postmodern Sophistications: Philosophy, Architecture, and Tradition* (Chicago: University of Chicago Press, 1990).

12. See Brian Vickers, *In Defence of Rhetoric* (Oxford: Clarendon Press, 1988), an invaluable text for the history of rhetoric. For a more thoughtful consideration than Vickers's of what rhetoric means, see Gerald L. Bruns's *Inventions: Writing,*

Textuality, and Understanding in Literary History (New Haven: Yale University Press, 1982), esp. pp. 1–13; and Hans Blumenberg, "An Anthropological Approach to the Contemporary Significance of Rhetoric," in *After Philosophy: End or Transformation?* ed. Kenneth Baynes, James Bohman, and Thomas McCarthy (Cambridge: MIT Press, 1987), pp. 429–58.

13. Jencks, *Architecture Today*, pp. 112–13. I think Portoghesi would approve of the rhetorical and hermeneutical turns I give to postmodernism, for he attends to rhetoric and demonstrates interest in the dialogical, as does Gadamer. As Portoghesi says, "Borromini . . . considers his profession as a formidable instrument of apprehension. . . . He uses every means for speaking with his interlocutor" (p. viii). In his conclusion, Portoghesi speaks of Borromini searching for liberation from "an autonomous purity that reduced [architecture's] communicative possibilities" (p. 391). Both quotations are from Barbara Luigia La Penta's translation of Portoghesi's *The Rome of Borromini* (New York: George Braziller, 1968). For Gadamer on architecture, see his "*Über das Lesen von Bauen und Bildern,*" in *Mödernität und Tradition: Festschrift für Max Imdahl zum 60. Gerburtstag,* ed. Gottfried Boehm, Karlheinz Stierle, Gundolf Winter (Munich: Wilhelm Fink Verlag, 1985), pp. 97–103.

14. Paolo Portoghesi, *Postmodern: The Architecture of Postindustrial Society* (New York: Rizzoli, 1983), p. 15. Unlike literary and philosophical postmodernists, Portoghesi writes repeatedly about communication rather than the undermining of discourse. He says, "The Postmodern in Architecture can therefore be read overall as a reemergence of archetypes, or as a reintegration of architectonic conventions, and thus as a premise to the creation of an architecture of communication, an architecture of the image for a civilization of the image" (p. 11).

15. Vincent Farenga, "Periphrasis on the Origin of Rhetoric," *Modern Language Notes* 94 (December 1979): 1035. Farenga is quoting from *Prolegomenon sylloge,* ed. Hugo Rabe (Leipzig: Teubner, 1931).

16. Ibid., p. 1036.

17. Hans-Georg Gadamer, *Truth and Method,* 2d rev. ed., trans. Joel Weinsheimer and Donald G. Marshall (New York: Crossroad Publishing, 1989), p. 103.

18. For a better understanding of Gadamer's view of play, see his chapter, "Play As the Clue to Ontological Explanation" in Ibid., pp. 101–34.

19. Jacques Derrida, *The Archeology of the Frivolous: Reading Condillac,* trans. John P. Leavey, Jr. (Pittsburgh: Duquesne University Press, 1980), p. 125.

20. Hans Blumenberg, *Work on Myth,* trans. Robert M. Wallace (Cambridge: MIT Press, 1985), p. 17.

21. Derrida, *Archeology of the Frivolous,* p. 127.

22. Richard Bernstein, "The New Skepticism" (Lecture delivered at the University of Iowa, March 9, 1987).

23. Maurice Blanchot, *The Space of Literature,* trans. Ann Smock (Lincoln: University of Nebraska Press, 1982), p. 109.

24. Gadamer, *Truth and Method,* p. 108.

25. Ihab Hassan, "Making Sense: The Trials of Postmodern Discourse," *New Literary History* 18 (Winter 1987): 445.

26. Vickers, *In Defence of Rhetoric,* p. viii.

27. Gerald L. Bruns, "Language and Power," *Chicago Review* (Spring 1984): 29.

28. Gadamer, *Truth and Method,* p. 462.

29. Craig Owens, "The Allegorical Impulse: Toward a Theory of Postmodernism," *October* 12 (Spring 1980): 67–86; and "The Allegorical Impulse (Part 2)," *October* 13 (Summer 1980): 59–80. Gregory L. Ulmer's "The Object of Post-Criticism" has a section dealing with allegory as well. See this essay in Foster's *The Anti-Aesthetic,* pp. 83–110. For more on allegory, see Jon Whitman's *Allegory: The Dynamics of an Ancient and Medieval Technique* (Cambridge: Harvard University Press, 1987).

30. Stephen Melville, "Notes on the Reemergence of Allegory, the Forgetting of Modernism, and the Necessity of Rhetoric, and the Conditions of Publicity in Art and Criticism," *October* 19 (Winter 1981): 59.

31. Gadamer, *Truth and Method,* p. 72.

32. Gyorgy Lukacs, *Realism in Our Times: Literature and the Class Struggle,* trans. John Mander and Necke Mander (New York, 1964), p. 40.

33. Bruns, *Inventions,* p. 6.

34. Franz Kafka, "In the Penal Colony," in *The Penal Colony: Stories and Short Pieces,* trans. Willa and Edwin Muir (New York: Schocken Books, 1948), p. 202.

35. Owens, "The Allegorical Impulse," p. 70.

36. For more on Icarus, see Joseph Leo Koerner's *Die Suche nach dem Labyrinth* (Frankfurt: Suhrkamp, 1983). Also see William Fisher's "Of Living Machines and Living-Machines: *Blade Runner* and the Terminal Genre," in *New Literary History* 20 (Autumn 1988): 187–98. Fisher includes *Brazil* in the "Terminal Genre," which he says "aims precisely at letting us lose our way in [a] labyrinth."

37. Theodor Adorno, *Minima Moralia: Reflections from Damaged Life,* trans. E.F.N. Jephcott (London: Verso, 1984), p. 115.

38. Gadamer, *Relevance of the Beautiful,* p. 64.

39. Pauline Kael, Review of *Brazil, The New Yorker,* February 10, 1986, p. 106.

40. Television sets are everywhere in *Brazil.* For example, the workers at the Department of Records use their computer terminals as television sets. One of the films they watch is *Casablanca,* about people trying to escape from a state, but who lack the proper papers. Having the proper papers is a major problem for characters in *Brazil,* especially for Jill Layton when she tries to reclaim Mr. Buttle's body. For more about *Casablanca* as precursor to postmodern collage, see Umberto Eco, "*Casablanca:* Cult Movies and Intertextual Collage," in *Travels in Hyperreality* (New York: Harcourt Brace Jovanovich, 1986), pp. 197–211.

41. See Leslie Bennetts, "How Terry Gilliam Found a Happy Ending for *Brazil,*" *The New York Times,* January 19, 1986, p. 16, "Arts and Entertainment" section.

42. Vicki Hearne, *Adam's Task: Calling Animals by Name* (New York: Alfred A. Knopf, 1986), p. 135.

43. Maurice Blanchot, *The Writing of the Disaster,* trans. Ann Smock (Lincoln: University of Nebraska Press, 1986), p. 1.

44. For further information on Eisenstein, see David A. Cook, *A History of*

Narrative Film (New York: W. W. Norton, 1981), pp. 142–81. Cook also includes reproductions of the Odessa steps sequence and the "masks of the gods" montage.

45. Norman Swallow, *Eisenstein: A Documentary Portrait* (New York, 1977), pp. 55–56.

46. Jean-François Lyotard, *The Postmodern Condition: A Report on Knowledge*, trans. Geoff Bennington and Brian Massumi (Minneapolis: University of Minnesota Press, 1984), p. 82. On the death of the social, see Arthur Kroker and David Cook, "Postmodernism and the Death of the Social," in *The Postmodern Scene: Excremental Culture and Hyper-Aesthetics* (New York: St. Martin's Press, 1986), pp. 168–242.

47. Felix Guattari, "The Postmodern Dead End," *Flash Art* 128 (May/June 1986): 40. This is a short but powerful critique of Lyotard and postmodernism in general.

48. Kael, Review of *Brazil*, p. 110. To learn more about *Brazil*, see Jack Mathews, *The Battle of "Brazil"* (New York: Crown, 1987). *Brazil* became the focus of bureaucratic pressures, mainly from Universal Studios, which wanted to turn the film into a futuristic romance with a happy ending. The story of the struggle between Gilliam and Universal is described in great detail in Mathews's book. To give *Brazil* the potential for commercial success, the functionaries at Universal suggested many changes in the film for its release in the United States in 1985. (*Brazil* had been released earlier in Europe.) For instance, Sidney Scheinberg, one of the major functionaries opposed to Gilliam's version, proposed a change in the film's score. "In my mind," Scheinberg said, "I still believe that a radical change in music utilizing appropriate contemporary recordings might be important in achieving audience interest in the all-important teenage category." Also, Universal suggested 37 different titles for the American version of *Brazil*, among them: *The Ball Bearing Electro Memory Circuit Buster; Arresting Developments; Chaos; Progress;* and *Gnu Yak, Gnu Yak and Other Bestial Places*. Without changing the title, Universal made $4 million from film rentals, and according to Mathews's sources, the studio will "just about break even" on *Brazil*, which cost about $15 million to make.

49. Lyotard, *Postmodern Condition*, p. 67.

50. Hans-Georg Gadamer, *Reason in the Age of Science*, trans. Frederick Lawrence (Cambridge: MIT Press, 1981), p. 73.

51. Gadamer, *Reason*, p. 74.

52. Rosen, *Hermeneutics*, p. 6.

Index